FROM HERE TO SERENITY

FROM HERE TO SERENITY

Four Principles for Understanding
Who You Really Are

JANE NELSEN

PRIMA PUBLISHING
3000 Lava Ridge Court • Roseville, California 95661
(800) 632-8676 • www.primalifestyles.com

PRIMA PUBLISHING and colophon are registered trademarks of Prima Communications Inc. registered with the United States Patent and Trademark Office.

Illustrations by Paula Gray

Cartoons on Pages 24, 37, 49, and 186 reprinted by permission of Chuck Vadun

Library of Congress Cataloging-in-Publication Data on File

ISBN 0-7615-2419-3

00 01 02 03 04 HH 10 9 8 7 6 5 4 3 2 1

Printed in the United States of America

HOW TO ORDER

Single copies may be ordered from Prima Publishing, 3000 Lava Ridge Court, Roseville, CA 95661; telephone (800) 632-8676. Quantity discounts are also available. On your letterhead, include information concerning the intended use of the books and the number of books you wish to purchase.

Visit us online at www.primalifestyles.com

To my children, Teryl, Jim, Ken, Brad, Lisa, Mark, and Mary, who are my continuing source of joy

CONTENTS

FOREWORD

It is not an exaggeration to say that the book you are holding changed my life and, consequently, the lives of literally hundreds of my clients and students over the last several years. When I first was introduced to this book, I had been teaching and counseling for many years. I believed that I was a successful therapist when I helped my clients "cope" with their problems. After all, I was pretty good at "coping" myself.

The first edition of *From Here to Serenity*, which was titled *Understanding*, threw me into my heart, where my own healing continued like I would never have imagined possible. I have found this to be true for many of the people I have counseled and taught since that time. I have suggested to my clients that one can't read this work just once or twice. It is a lifetime process of struggling to stay in the *heart*. This book, written for the layman, takes me back into my heart every time I read it. I have reviewed this revision several times and can say with complete honesty that it is better than ever in achieving this end.

The science of the Psychology of Mind evolved out of the 1980s. The followers seemed to be a strange mix of mystics and board-certified psychologists. After thoroughly digesting Dr. Nelsen's book, my enthusiasm and personal results from her work drove me to send for and study in depth all of the material I could get my hands on that explained this new science. I soon discovered that there is nothing out there for the ordinary person that comes close to explaining the principles and precepts of this remarkable science as does *Understanding*.

We seem to have an imbalance leaning toward the "head" in our culture, which makes it very difficult to find lasting joy and satisfaction in all of our relationships. The programmed thought system generates our mental, and most of our physical, ills. It is not easy for those of us who were raised in our thought-dominated culture to grasp the concept of being able to stand back objectively and view how the brain works. "Not able to see the forest for the trees" is more than just a cliché when it comes to trying to understand ourselves and why we *think* and thus act the way we do. *Understanding*, in my experience, helps create this new awareness as nothing else in literature is able to do.

I have found that understanding my dysfunction in relationships is, however, only part of the healing equation. There are many practitioners and hoards of books on the market right now that do a wonderful job of helping us see where our emotional problems came from. I agree with Dr. Nelsen that some of this information can be extremely helpful. These excellent works can open the doors for personal growth when used to help people heal old beliefs from the past that block them from accessing their hearts, their inner wisdom, their spiritual source. However, after years of experience, I have found that for a complete life change—a rebirth, if you will—to take place in a person's life, something more than just getting in touch with the reasons for their dysfunction needs to occur. This is where the principles taught in *Understanding* have had such great impact.

In clear, precise, understandable dialogue, Dr. Nelsen is able to make it easy to get out of the thought system, which creates all dysfunction, and into the heart, where *real* emotional and behavioral change can begin to take place. Rereading the chapters creates this change effortlessly, even as I read.

Especially helpful are the latter chapters, which contain clear, realistic life experience examples where changing the heart can change the outcomes of previous relationship breakdowns. It seems that emotions are some of the most misunderstood and feared of all constructs within the field of psychology. Understanding that emotions are created instantaneously from feelings and learning that I have control over my feelings is one of the greatest breakthroughs in the study of "mind" in the twentieth century. My feelings are totally different when I am in my heart than when I am in my programmed thought system.

A well-known actor recently stated publicly that self-help books had changed his life and that he lived on a steady diet of them. I can personally understand why he could make such a remark. People who are seeking to grow and who are willing to pay the price for that growth will eventually find the way. However, as I have often told my seminar students, you could take away every book I have but one, the one you are now holding, and I could still maintain my own emotional health and love of life. I share with them the honest fact that the equation for personal happiness and contentment in my own life shifted dramatically from a twenty percent happy/eighty percent coping state to a realistic ninety percent happy/ten percent coping state, simply from being introduced to her book many years ago.

Someone said once, "If we continue to do what we've always done, we'll always get what we've always got." Our culture has always enthroned the head or intellect as our master and doggedly insisted on trying to solve all of our problems with it, not realizing that *it* is the problem. My great hope and dream for the future of mental health in our world is that with renewed "Understanding" we can do something different and thus start reaping better emotional rewards—in other words, "change our *hearts*." This book is more than just a start; it is the very "*way*."

MERRILL J. BAILEY, M.ED.

INTRODUCTION
AND ACKNOWLEDGMENTS

This book was first self-published under the title *Under-standing: Eliminating Stress and Dissatisfaction in Life and Relationships*. I was totally surprised that so many copies (30,000) sold as a self-published book. The sales were due, in part, to the word-of-mouth popularity among "recovery" organizations in Minneapolis. For this reason, when Prima decided to publish the book, the title was changed to *Under-standing, Eliminating Stress and Finding Serenity in Life and Relationships*. Of course, the sales were much greater with the help of Prima.

So, why another edition? People kept telling me the book needed a better title—one that was more understand-able than *Understanding*. It is my hope that the theme of the book will be more obvious through its current title.

There are changes in this edition, but they are minor. I am always humbled when I read this book myself (which I must do carefully when revising). Each page takes me to my serenity at a deeper level than usual. I bought a brand-new laptop computer in the middle of the revision. I dropped it and cracked the LDC screen, which cost almost as much to repair as the original cost. And negligence isn't covered in the warranty. Still, I couldn't get very upset. When I tried, I would see my "drama" and couldn't get away with it. It is true that circumstances cannot upset us—only what we think about the circumstances. Since I can get caught up in my thought system as well as anyone else, I read this book often. It always takes me back to my heart and an understanding of who I really am and what is truly important in life—the peace I once searched for in workshop after workshop.

I was once a workshop junkie. I used to wonder in jest if I would ever find the last workshop—one that would finally teach me the magic techniques that would give me enough competence and confidence to be truly helpful to myself and others. I never found what I was looking for. Instead, I found something better—principles that taught me where competence, confidence, and wisdom are and always have been—within myself. I had read and heard, over and over, the advice to go within, but I didn't know how to do it.

The intellectual knowledge that "the kingdom of heaven is within" and "as a man thinketh, so is he" was not new to me, but I had never experienced these truths. I finally discovered a seminar where principles were explained that led me to experience my inner kingdom of happiness and peace of mind. I gratefully acknowledge and give thanks to George Pransky and Robert Kausen, who put up with my "what ifs" and "yes, buts" until I was finally able to hear at a deeper level.

After experiencing such dramatic results in my life from what I learned from George Pransky and Robert Kausen, I felt inspired to spend six months in fellowship at the Advanced Human Studies Institute in Coral Gables, Florida. Studying and working with Dr. Rick Suarez and Dr. Kimberly Kiddoo was truly a beautiful and enriching experience. What a privilege it was to be led to a deeper understanding of inner resources via the wisdom of these pioneers and innovators of the Psychology of Mind.

I originally intended to write this book with Kimberly Kiddoo because she was such an inspiration to me. When she decided not to coauthor the book, she encouraged me to use some of her examples because, as she said, "*Understanding the examples makes them your own, and getting this out in a book will help so many people.*" I miss her. Dr. Kiddoo is now in private practice in Coral Gables.

It is with loving appreciation that I acknowledge Dr. William Pettit, a prominent psychiatrist who dropped his successful practice and position as a national trainer of a popular growth seminar when he heard the principles of Psychology of Mind. He moved his family to Florida and was finishing his fellowship at the Advanced Human Studies Institute while I was there. I am filled with gratitude as I remember his delightful influence, which is reflected in this book. Dr. Pettit wanted to find a "quiet" place to practice psychiatry and now lives in Aberdeen, South Dakota.

It was a special thrill to receive an endorsement from Wayne Dyer. His books and tapes have been an inspiration to me and my family for years. His book *Gifts from Eykis* (New York: Pocket Books, 1983) is a special gift for those of us who enjoy laughing while we learn profound truths. Wayne continues to inspire me as he "comes out of the closet" with profound spiritual teachings through his new books and lectures.

Because my desire was to be instrumental in helping others experience the joy and serenity found in understanding the principles of Psychology of Mind, it has been a gratifying and humbling experience to hear from so many people who have read the first edition of this book. That so many would be touched was beyond my comprehension, and I hope that many more will find serenity through this revised edition.

One reason for the previous revision was the discovery of additional concepts that deepened my level of understanding. That new understanding led me to revise my belief that one should never go into the past. Thanks to Valerie Seeman Moreton and Max Skousen, I learned healing processes for going into the past that helped me heal some beliefs that were beyond by awareness. It now seems like common sense to understand that sometimes we need to heal the beliefs we created as part of our thought systems. Too often these beliefs filter our life experience even when we are not consciously aware of them. Healing is effective and powerful when it is based on an understanding of the four principles discussed in this book.

The gratitude I feel for Jack and Deborah Bartello feels sacred to me. They came into my life immediately after the first edition of *Understanding* was self-published. They gently introduced me (kicking and screaming all the way) to a beautiful, spiritual world that was unattainable through my thought system. In fact, it is my thought system that did all the kicking and screaming. I recently asked them how they were able to put up with my resistance. They said simply, "There is not any resistance in your energy. We pay more attention to energy than any other communication." Their influence is intricately woven throughout this book.

My good friend, Dr. Bill Hutcherson, has been my "workshop junkie" buddy for years. We no longer tolerate the workshops that give validity to the thought system but still enjoy workshops that take us to our hearts and spiritual sources. He suggested some deletions in the last edition that I didn't understand until they got past my thought system. He is ever gentle with his suggestions.

I am especially grateful to my husband, Barry. He is one of the most unconditionally loving people I know. It was the healing of some subconscious beliefs that has allowed me to accept and appreciate his love. Through *understanding* we have learned, even when we get into the insanity of our programmed thought systems, to be kind to each other until we learn from the experience or until it passes.

I do not want to give the impression that life is always total bliss. We are on this planet to learn and to grow. Every experience gives us opportunities for learning and growing at whatever depth we choose. All the principles discussed in *From Here to Serenity* have helped me view both "good" and "bad" experiences with gratitude—sooner or later. You will understand why after reading this book.

My next acknowledgment is to my children, to whom this book is dedicated. We continually love and learn from one another. My daughter Mary made a statement that sums up the value of the principles discussed in this book. I got lost for a short time in feelings of insecurity and was behaving irrationally. Because of my *understanding* of the four principles, it didn't last too long. Mary later said, "I knew you would soon realize what you were doing, Mom."

And, last but not least, I want to thank my editors at Prima, Jamie Miller and Shawn Vreeland, for their help, encouragement, and availability.

It is my hope that *From Here to Serenity* will help you understand what you are doing, learn from it, and quickly return to your heart, where you will experience joy and serenity.

CHAPTER ONE

Are You Afraid of Serenity?

D o you think it would be boring to have serenity? Do you equate serenity with nonproductivity? Are you afraid that the only way you could have serenity is to give up everything you have accomplished or learned?

If you answer yes to any of these questions, you do not understand serenity. Serenity is not what you think—literally, as you will see in chapter 4. Serenity is what you already are but have buried under layers of thought system thinking.

Serenity comes from the Latin *serenus*, which means clear, cloudless, untroubled. It does not mean stagnation, nor does it mean total passivity. In fact, serenity is the birthplace for creativity, wisdom, and meaningful productivity. And what, you may ask, is meaningful productivity?

You would have to tell me. It is whatever is truly meaningful to the real you—the you that is now buried under tons of false meaning. *From Here to Serenity* takes you from the "here" of your false meaning—the meaning that has been created in your thought system—to the serenity of your true meaning.

When you rediscover your serenity, you will not be bored. It is unlikely that you will be spending your whole day meditating in the lotus position. You will not be in constant quiet seclusion. Instead, you will have deep awareness that may give you joy or compassion, gratitude, wisdom, and an understanding of your true self and your true purpose.

You won't lack productivity. You will know exactly what to do—for the "right" reasons. You will not be scurrying around to fill some vague void. You will have nothing to prove. You will no longer be a slave to your ego or to the ego of others. You will listen to others with interest, but not as a measure of who you are. You will stop worshiping the god of "what do you think of me?" From a state of serenity, you will have access to your inner wisdom.

Does this sound too good to be true? Well, it could be. I can't promise you that you will be able to maintain a state of serenity all the time. I don't. Perhaps the human experience was not designed for total serenity. However, I believe it is a deep desire of the human spirit to find serenity (peace). An understanding of the principles described in this book can guide you to a state of serenity any time you choose—under any circumstances.

Recently, I experienced a huge loss. My stomach was in knots for several hours. In the past, this would have led to fear, self-flagellation for my mistakes, and deep depression. Instead, I remembered my understanding of the principles in this book and felt gratitude instead of depression. Instead of focusing on the loss, I focused on other gifts, both spiritually and earthly. I will be forever grateful for the principles that taught me to understand who I really am and what has true value. I look forward to sharing these principles with you.

CHAPTER TWO

A Treasure Map

How are you living your life? Are you so busy (which seems to be the trend in our society) that you haven't even noticed or thought about the direction of your life? Are you aware that how you live your life is your creation and that you have a choice about how it will be? Do you have peace of mind and serenity; or do you live in stress, anxiety, dissatisfaction, disappointment, anger, or depression? Hopefully, you aren't one of the thousands who use antidepressants, illegal drugs, and alcohol—a pervasive problem in our society even though people who rely on drugs find only momentary relief.

Or are you one of the many who expect to find happiness through material objects, power, or other people, only to become addicted to the need for more—more power, another relationship, more *things*? Materialism and the attempt to feed the starving ego through power, things, or relationships are other detours from serenity and peace of mind. People who take these routes often end up asking, "Is that all there is?"

Perhaps you (along with millions) are caught up in the rat race of trying to prove your worth—worshiping the god of "what do you think of me?" As you read this, do you see the insanity of it all? Do you wonder why anyone would choose any of these crazy lifestyles? Yet most of us do. Why do we do this? Why do we continue to do things when, at some level, we know better—when we have heard it all before?

An abundance of wisdom about happiness and peace of mind is available through spoken and written words. You may have experienced inspiration from beautiful words of wisdom and vowed to be better and then felt disappointed when you did not maintain those inspired feelings. Perhaps you have found that sometimes, even though you remembered what you should do, you just didn't feel able to do it. You may have had times when you felt like giving in to feelings of discouragement, failure, and self-blame. Then you may have felt inspired to do better again—only to repeat the cycle.

How can you remain inspired so that words of wisdom are truly helpful in your life, instead of remaining mere "shoulds" that you feel you can't live up to? What does it take to understand words of wisdom and integrate them into your being at such a deep level that living in serenity, joy, and gratitude becomes your normal state of mind? How can you keep to a minimum your lapses from this peaceful state of mind, learn from the situations life presents to you, and return to your natural state of happiness with a deeper understanding of your life purpose?

> Good feelings are natural in human beings, but often they are buried under the debris of negative thoughts taken too seriously (something most of us have become adept at).

This book explains four principles of psychological functioning[1] that show you how to access the inner wisdom and happiness you have heard so much about and have probably occasionally experienced. Surely you have heard it said that happiness is *within*, but do you *experience* what that means? Or do you keep looking outside yourself? Would you like to know how to stop the frantic search? If you are ready for serenity, the principles in this book provide the map that will lead you to the treasure—inside yourself.

Living in serenity and happiness comes from beautiful feelings inherent within each of us. These natural

---

1. Originally formulated by Rick Suarez, Ph.D., and Roger C. Mills, Ph.D., *Sanity, Insanity, and Common Sense: The Groundbreaking New Approach to Happiness* (New York: Ballantine, Fawcett Columbine, 1987). Out of print.

good feelings get buried under our programmed thought system. When our inherent good feelings are uncovered, we live naturally in a happy, loving state of being. The kingdom of heaven *is* within.

You may not believe that you have inherent good feelings of joy, wisdom, and peace—or you may believe it but feel frustrated that you can't access these feelings. You may feel blocked and imprisoned within your own mind—as indeed you are when you don't understand how a programmed thought system works and how to get beyond it. An understanding of the four principles can open the prison doors. These principles (discussed in chapters 4 through 7) serve as a treasure map to *the kingdom of heaven within.* Once you *understand* these principles, you can access the treasures buried deep within you—anytime you choose.

Inherent good feelings are like corks in water, naturally bobbing to the surface unless weighted down or buried under debris. Good feelings are natural in human beings, but often they are buried under the debris of negative thoughts taken too seriously (something most of us have become adept at). An *understanding* of the four principles removes the weights and the debris so that wisdom, gratitude, and peaceful feelings can bob to the top.

Even though happiness, joy, and serenity are inherent within everyone (as will be explained in chapter 4), life presents many lessons for you to learn. Once you understand this, you can be open to the lessons instead of being paralyzed by fear, anxiety, or anger when you encounter opportunities to learn. In later chapters, you will learn how to see problems as friends with wonderful life messages. As you learn to recognize this possibility, the fear, anxiety, and anger vanish while the messages remain.

This does not mean that you will live in total bliss all the time. Because of the programmed thought system you have created (as discussed in chapter 3), it is normal to get hooked into old programming and become lost in your illusions. This is why a treasure map provided by the four principles is such a liberating gift. You can always find your way back home—to your inherent good feelings.

How can I make such claims? It is because an understanding of the principles has been such a gift in my own life and in the lives of friends, clients, and other therapists who have come to understand them. Even when we get lost in our thought systems for a while, there is a sense of knowing that we have simply sidetracked ourselves by taking our thoughts seriously. We don't stay sidetracked for long when we understand what we are doing. Being stuck for prolonged periods lets us know that we may need help healing some inaccurate, deeply embedded beliefs. However, all healing processes are enhanced when based on an understanding of the four principles.

Understanding the principles has increased my understanding of everything and has taken me beyond an intellectual belief in the wonderful words of wisdom I have heard over the years to an *experience* of their meaning. Now, instead of knowing that it must be true that the kingdom of heaven is within, I can experience this wonderful state of being anytime I choose to follow the treasure map created by the four principles.

This does not mean I never get off course into un-happiness, but the principles show me exactly how I got off course and point me back in the direction of my in-herent good feelings. Like any often-used map, the direc-tion soon becomes so natural that it is easier to find the way without a map. However, just as detours can take us away from a familiar road, we often find ourselves in a detour away from our inherent peace of mind. A pro-grammed thought system is much more complex than a highway system. Ruts and sinkholes (old buried decisions and beliefs) often hook us and lead us astray.

Perhaps we are not truly being led astray; it could be part of a perfect plan that we experience separation from serenity so that we can learn more life lessons. One of the reasons for revising this book is that I have learned to ap-preciate the value of the lessons and gifts that can be found in "detours." This decreases my tendency to beat up on myself when my understanding isn't sufficient or permanent.

I'm sure you have noticed that some people get very angry when they have to take a highway detour. Others, however, see detours as an adventure and an opportunity to discover something new. People who don't find the gifts and lessons in their life experiences often stay angry, get depressed, or act like victims. Life becomes a matter of coping instead of occasions for joy and discovery.

Perhaps you have been well trained in effective coping skills. This can be very helpful because coping is certainly better than not coping. It brings only temporary relief, however, until the next problem arises. Coping is like bailing water when you don't know how to plug the hole in the boat. (Of course, bailing is much better than sinking.)

The exciting news is that the four basic principles show you how to plug the hole, how to reseal the boat. You don't need to learn how to *cope* with stress or anxiety; you can eliminate these states of mind whenever you want to. This book gives many examples of common situations in life and relationships that illustrate how a problem can be eliminated through an *understanding* of the four principles.

Someone once asked, "So, what is the point of all this?"

My answer: "To be happy."

Too many people get caught up in the search for happiness and forget to be happy. I say "forget" because you already know how to be happy, but the knowledge is buried, unused. Buried knowledge is like a well-kept secret.

A client recently said to me, "Well, sure you're happy. Look at all you have."

I replied, "That's the point. I had everything I have now before I learned about these principles, and I still wasn't happy." I paid more attention to my illusions of insecurity and a false need to prove myself than to my inherent feelings of gratitude, joy, wisdom, and love.

This explains why so many people who have achieved fame, fortune, or other forms of success as defined by our society are often dissatisfied, whereas others who have little may be quite happy. Happiness has little to do with relationships, material possessions or achievements. Lasting happiness and peace of mind are found within, no matter what the circumstances.

In the following poem, Sue Petit has captured what happens when we listen softly from our hearts:

Coming Home[2]

Coming home to peace and quiet.
Coming home to feelings warm.
Coming home where there's a fullness,
    where love in me is born.
Coming home's a simple journey,
    takes no movement on my part.
Instead of listening to my thoughts,
I listen with my heart.

This treasure map is one of the most valuable gifts I have ever received. It has helped me find the buried treasure within myself. It is my hope that it will help you find lasting peace of mind and happiness within yourself.

Happy treasure hunting!

---

2. Sue Petit, *Coming Home* (Fair Oaks, CA: Sunrise Press). This book of poems, which beautifully and humorously illustrate the four principles of Psychology of Mind, can be ordered by calling (605) 226-3326.

CHAPTER THREE

Listening Softly

As you read this book, listen softly. Listen "from your heart," for insight, for a feeling within that lets you hear truth. In our society, we have been taught to pay more attention to the logic of our intellects than to our hearts. Deepak Chopra suggests another possibility in his book *The Seven Spiritual Laws of Success:*

> Only the heart knows the correct answer. Most people think the heart is mush and sentimental. But it's not. The heart is intuitive; it's holistic, it's contextual, it's relational. It doesn't have a win-lose orientation. It taps into the cosmic computer— the field of pure potentiality, pure knowledge, and infinite organizing power—and takes everything into account. At times it may not even seem rational, but the heart has a computing ability that is far more accurate and far more precise than anything within the limits of rational thought.[1]

Listening for an insight from the heart is very different from listening from the intellect.[2] The brain has

---

1. Deepak Chopra, *The Seven Laws of Spiritual Success* (San Rafael: Amber-Allen Publishing & New World Library, 1994), pp. 43–44.
2. This is a good definition of what I mean by *understanding*. It is that feeling of inspiration or insight that takes you into the realm of your heart or spiritual source. *Understanding* is a spiritual experience, not an intellectual experience.

unlimited capacity and capabilities. However, we have limited our brains with a thought system "programmed" with old decisions based on mistaken interpretations that became solid beliefs, which are then seen as reality. This programmed thought system filters any new possibilities, including the truth; it tries to fit everything into what it already knows—or rejects it.

Listen softly for a feeling insight because words are inadequate to express love, beauty, principle, or any other intangible truth. These truths can be understood only through the personal experience of them, which is beyond words. Someone once asked Louis Armstrong to explain jazz. He replied, "If you can't feel it, I don't know how I can explain it." The only purpose of words in this book is to point you toward the kind of *understanding* you will feel in your heart. If you can't feel it, you will not *understand* it.

We often focus on words and miss the feeling being expressed. Each person hears words from his or her own frame of reference and interpretation. For example, your mental picture of a dog is different from that of your friends' mental picture. This is why discussions of religion and politics are often avoided; these topics trigger so many differing beliefs and emotions about what is "right" and "wrong" that we stop listening.

Insight from the heart often can make the traditional definition of words seem topsy-turvy. For example, I once believed that forgiveness meant I should do something noble from my intellect. Through *understanding*, forgiveness becomes a nonissue. When I drop my judgments and move into my heart, there is nothing to forgive. Forgiveness feels more like an awareness of the

truth about my illusions, or a feeling of compassion, than something to *do*. You will find many examples yourself of how meanings change as you understand the principles.

Listening softly—listening from your heart and inner wisdom instead of your head—helps you get past the limitation of words. Words can sound hollow and intellectual, whereas the experience of what the words are trying to convey can be so full. The gap between the two is bridged by the understanding that comes from insight. Some people get goose bumps when they have the experience of knowing, from deep within, that they are hearing the truth. Others have a knowing that feels like it comes from the heart (or intuition or spiritual source) even when it may not make sense to the intellect. Just about everyone has had the experience of having an insight that seems to come from nowhere—especially when they couldn't figure something out after *thinking* about it.

The principles, soon to be explained, help you remember how to bypass the limits of your programmed thought system so that you can experience insight. I say "remember" because you were born with that capability and used it as a child to enjoy your life, to learn, and to experience many beautiful things. Insight is a recognition of a principle or truth that eludes you when you are stuck in the rigid patterns of your thought system.

Remember when you were trying to learn math principles? At first it did not matter how many times you added 2 + 2; it didn't really make sense. Then, suddenly, you caught on and could add any combination of numbers. It made sense that 5 + 7 was the same as 7 + 5. This is one example of experiencing insight to understand a principle. Learning to ride a bicycle or walk a balance beam in gymnastics are other examples. No matter how many times you heard an explanation of the concept of balance, it was beyond your comprehension until you experienced it for yourself.

Most of us kept plugging away at math and practicing balance, even when the principles made no sense to us. We had to trust that we would eventually learn. Some of us may have practiced out of love for the teacher rather than from faith in future results. Others may have developed a belief that they could not learn and may still have "blocks" about math or balance.

The principles of math and balance do not provide answers. They simply show you how to find answers or how to discover mistakes and make corrections. The principles explained in this book show you how to find answers and make corrections in your life.

As you read, notice how difficult it can be to hear and understand the principles when you listen only with your intellect. You will know you are in touch with your inner wisdom and inspiration when you read something and have that "aha" feeling—or, upon reading something you disagree with, instead of having negative feelings you are led to a higher understanding that makes more sense to you than the words in this book.

At times you may say with irritation, "But I have heard that before" or "I already know that." When you have "really" heard it at an insight level, you do not get irritated at hearing it again—you feel reaffirmed.

People often hear principles intellectually with just enough understanding to give them lip service. When they *understand*, they give heart service. Lip service often includes "shoulds" and "shouldn'ts," or ego gratification. Heart service comes from inner joy, gratitude, and an unconditional desire to be of service to others.

> Understanding is the key to natural happiness and serenity. *Insight* from within is the key to understanding. *Listening softly* for a feeling is the key to insight.

Reading this book could be like putting together a puzzle. Sometimes one piece makes no sense until it fits with another. Perhaps something you read in the middle or at the end will give you the insight to make the beginning more understandable.

This book is short so that it will be easy to read many times. If you get even a glimmer of *understanding* the first time, you will get more each time you read. Your reading experience will be different as your understanding deepens. When your understanding is deep enough, it will automatically override your limited, programmed thought system, and you will access your inherent good feelings and inner wisdom. Several people have told me that they keep this book on their bedside table and reread parts at random. They say, "I always seem to choose just the section I need to help me through whatever I am struggling with at the time."

Most of your questions will be answered as you keep reading. The answers will come not from what you read but from the insight you experience from your own inner wisdom. The purpose of this book is to help you regain greater access to these sources within yourself.

Understanding is the key to natural happiness and serenity.

Insight from within is the key to understanding.

Listening softly for a feeling is the key to insight.

This is the cycle. It doesn't matter where you start; each aspect leads in the same direction for positive results in your life and relationships. You are reading this book because you hope to eliminate stress and find serenity, joy, happiness, and peace of mind. Like math and balance, before understanding, principles can seem complicated. After understanding, they seem beautifully simple. When you hear the principles in your heart, you will *understand;* and you will experience *serenity* in your life.

Keep listening softly.

CHAPTER FOUR

The Principle of Thinking As a Function

Y ou think! This is the best-kept secret of all. *Under-standing* that you think is the key to understanding everything else in life.

You may be saying, "That's not a secret. Everyone knows he or she thinks." Actually, very few people remember that thinking is a function or an ability. Instead, they believe that what they think is reality. Most act as though they are passive receivers—or victims—of their thoughts rather than creators.

In the movie *2001*, scientists create a very sophisticated computer for their space mission. This computer has so many human qualities that it is named Hal. Hal is an amazing servant until, through its human qualities, it develops an ego. Hal stops being a servant and takes over the spaceship.

Truth can be stranger than fiction. Humans have an amazing brain that can act as an amazing tool. However, through conditioning, we all create a programmed thought system and an ego. The trouble begins when we forget it is our creation and allow it to become our master. The plot thickens when we don't even know we have become servants of a heartless master. We become allies or victims of the misery caused by our programmed thought system by believing in it. We believe in it only when we don't understand that thinking is a function, not a reality.

In her book *A Return to Love*, Marianne Williamson confirms what happens when we forget that we created our own thought system and ego:

> Thought separated from love is a profound miscreation. It's our own power turned against ourselves. . . . The ego has a pseudo-life of its own, and like all life forms, fights hard for it's survival. . . . The ego is like a virus in the computer that attacks the core system.[1]

Thinking is an ability we use to create our reality. What we think determines what we see—even though we often make the mistake of believing, in an upside-down way, that what we see determines what we think. There is a popular saying, "I'll believe it when I see it." But the truth is reflected in the title of a book by Wayne Dyer, *You'll See It When You Believe It*.[2]

We can think anything we choose to think, and our emotions and actions are then a direct result of what we choose to think. (However, positive thinking is not the answer, as will be discussed later.) Any form of insecurity, stress, or anxiety results from creating thoughts that

---

1. Marianne Williamson, *A Return to Love* (New York: Harper Paperbacks, 1992), p. 35.
2. Wayne Dyer, *You'll See It When You Believe It* (New York: William Morrow, 1989).

produce those kinds of emotions and then believing those thoughts are reality rather than products of thinking.[3] For instance, try feeling insecure without thinking that you are insecure. It is impossible. As soon as you take the content of your thoughts seriously, you have forgotten that thinking is a function rather than reality.

To see this even more clearly, consider the following examples. Joe feels inadequate. He believes his inadequacy is real, and does not recognize it as just a thought. His inadequacy exists because he believes it is real; he bases his behavior on that thought and acts inadequate. (This is why it is not helpful simply to tell people they are adequate. Your belief does not change them. They will feel adequate only when they change their thoughts—or when they access their inner wisdom as discussed below.)

In our next example, Melissa believes she is depressed because life is overwhelming. But life itself is not overwhelming; only *what she thinks about life* makes it seem overwhelming. This statement can bring up all kinds of debate: "What about disasters, death, war, and so on?" The point I am making is illustrated by two people who experienced an earthquake. One was living in fear and trying to figure out how to move out of earthquake country. The other said, "This helped me realize what is important in life. I don't need all the things I lost in the earthquake. This event was a wake-up call for me to enjoy the more important things in my life, such as my

---

3. Actually, there are two levels of feelings: those that come from our thoughts and those that come from our heart or spiritual source. This is discussed further in chapter 4.

family and the simple pleasures of life." Some might say, "But what if she lost her family?" The point is illustrated again by two people who lost loved ones. One person went into depression and could not imagine living without her loved one. Another person said, "What a gift it was to have this person in my life for the time I had. I miss him terribly—and I will go on enjoying the many gifts life has to offer."

Many people argue that attitudes are not a product of thinking but of circumstances. If attitudes were a product of circumstances, however, it would be impossible to find people who still celebrate life even with terminal cancer or crippling afflictions. But there are many happy people who are experiencing all kinds of circumstances in life.

We are often touched and inspired by stories of people who swim without arms, ski without legs, "run" races in wheelchairs, start again after "failures," or celebrate life no matter what the circumstances. Conversely, we could be moved to compassion for people who quit celebrating life because they don't realize that through their thoughts they are making themselves more miserable than their circumstances warrant. It is never the events in our life that create our reality—it is our thoughts about the events.

Some people go through life with the attitude that life is a celebration—something to enjoy fully. Others have the attitude that life is a chore—something to be endured. There is a popular poster expressing this attitude: "Life is hard, and then you die."

Which is it? A celebration or a chore? The answer depends entirely upon what you think.

EXPERIENCING YOUR LIFE THROUGH YOUR THOUGHT SYSTEM OR HEART

Each person has a thought system for storing the memories, perceptions, judgments, and beliefs that act as filters, creating his or her unique, separate reality. (The

> It is the thought system that changes "the spirit of the law" to "the letter of the law."

principle of separate realities is discussed in chapter 6.) Years of accepting beliefs—yours and others'—creates the kind of conditioning that makes illusions seem like reality.[4]

Each individual also has a spiritual source through which he or she can experience wisdom, inspiration, and all the good feelings that are inherent in every human being. There are many names for this spiritual source. Some people call it inner wisdom. Others call it universal wisdom, Spirit, the higher self, the heart, or God. I will use the terms *heart* or *spiritual source* interchangeably or together.

Through your heart or spiritual source, you experience life in a way that is quite different from your mental perceptions. Through your heart, you see life freshly, moment to moment, with fascination, joy, and love—or at least simple acceptance of what is. But when you take thoughts from your thought system seriously, you block

---

4. This is not a condemnation of the thought system. It is a normal phenomenon created and experienced by all of us based on the interpretations and decisions we made as young children when we didn't have the capacity to do anything else. The purpose of this book is simply to help people *understand* the prisons of the mind they have created so they can be free.

your spiritual source and lose access to your inner wisdom and inspiration.

CONDITIONING

We start at an early age to create a thought system, which is made up of our own perceptions and interpretations as well as those we accept from others. We are very trusting when we are young, usually believing what anyone tells us. Unfortunately, much of what we are told consists of beliefs passed along from generation to generation. This is not done maliciously; our family and friends would not pass on troublesome beliefs if they knew what they were doing. Not knowing any better, they themselves accepted beliefs passed on to them when they were young. Not all beliefs that are passed on are harmful. Many come from the heart or spiritual source and are inherent in the beliefs of every culture: love, gratitude, forgiveness. These beliefs would be lived purely if they weren't contaminated by rigid beliefs and judgments from the thought system. It is the thought system that changes "the spirit of the law" to "the letter of the law."

Most of these beliefs passed on from generation to generation are full of "shoulds" and "shouldn'ts" that contain judgments of worth or worthlessness. We are told how we should be in order to be liked and to be successful. We are also told how others should be and how life should be. We, others, and life hardly ever fit these beliefs, so we live with failure, pseudo-success, anxiety,

What do you mean, you don't accept negative programming?

stress, or disappointment in ourselves, life, and others. Unlike the computer that won't accept negative programming in the cartoon above, our brain will.

Our thought systems also contain such helpful information and skills as reading, writing, arithmetic, names, phone numbers, and the like, which make life easier and more enjoyable. This information is factual and does not create emotions; we use it for our benefit rather than against ourselves.

It is the illusionary thoughts that get us into trouble when they create negative emotions and we believe they are reality. The beliefs and interpretations we accept or create can seem so real that we live and die for them, even when they make no sense. These beliefs and emotions are the source of hatred, prejudices, war, lack of forgiveness, and all insecurities.

CRAZY THOUGHTS—YOURS, NOT MINE

Illusionary thinking is often easier to see in other people than it is to see in ourselves. I remember thinking schizophrenics were really crazy when they thought they saw little green bugs crawling up the wall or when they believed they were Napoleon. It was obvious to me that those were crazy thoughts, whereas all my thoughts, naturally, were serious and real—even the ones that made me miserable.

One psychologist shared that, before she had a deeper understanding of these principles, she had a client in therapy who believed a garbage truck was going to eat her. The psychologist spontaneously laughed and said, "That is a silly thought." She had spoken from her common sense and wisdom but felt a little embarrassed because she had been taught that it is inappropriate to laugh at something a client is taking seriously. Fortunately, the client heard the truth of those words at an even deeper level than they had been spoken, and she began to improve significantly. Several months later the psychologist asked what had made the difference in her recovery. The client replied, "It was the day you told me my thoughts couldn't hurt me." (It wasn't really what the psychologist said but the insight that was inspired by the words.)

We all have silly thoughts we take seriously. Yet when we know they are just thoughts, they lose their power to hurt us.

CONTROLLING YOUR THOUGHTS IS NOT THE POINT

We have power over our programmed thought system when we *understand* it and dismiss it, not when we try to control it.

> When you realize that thinking is a function or an ability rather than a reality, you can be transformed immediately to your heart or spiritual source, where you feel and express your inherent wisdom and good feelings.

Dismissing our programmed thought system does not mean positive thinking. It does not mean denial. It does not mean repression. It means *understanding* that thinking is a function, a tool—not a reality. When we understand this, the thought system is automatically dismissed because we see the illusions of our beliefs. Through *understanding* we are automatically transformed because the thought system is dismissed, and our inherent good feelings, our hearts, our spiritual sources fill the vacuum.

One of my clients quit having panic attacks after hearing the above story about the garbage truck. She said, "The last time a panic attack started, I knew it was just my thoughts. I laughed and felt fine."

I know it is not this simple for everyone. It wasn't for me. Some people *understand* sooner than others. As I have said before, it seems so difficult until *understanding* makes it so simple.

THINKING AS AN EXPRESSION OF WISDOM FROM THE HEART VERSUS THINKING FROM THE THOUGHT SYSTEM

No one wants the misery created by negative thoughts. Yet some people seem to live as if they do, only because they do not understand the difference between thinking as an expression of wisdom from the heart and thinking as a reflex of fixed beliefs from their programmed thought system.

The next time you feel upset or miserable, notice what you are thinking. Your emotions are created by your thoughts. Taking your negative thoughts seriously simply means you have forgotten that you created them in the first place (often at a subconscious level).[5]

When you realize that thinking is a function or an ability rather than a reality, you can be transformed immediately to your heart or spiritual source, where you feel and express your inherent wisdom and good feelings. The first thing your inner wisdom will help you realize is how

---

5. Please see chapter 8 for more information about subconscious programming. It is often our subconscious programming that produces our present feelings. When this happens, it may appear that our thoughts are caused by our feelings instead of our feelings being caused by our thoughts.

funny it is to take negative thoughts seriously and to base your life on them.

Many have argued, "Good feelings are not natural to me. It is more natural for me to feel stressed or depressed. I don't try to feel these things; they are just naturally there." But they are not "just naturally" there. There is a negative thought behind every negative feeling.

Can you imagine the problems babies and young children would have if they tried to learn to walk and talk through insecurities produced by a programmed thought system? What would happen if they formed beliefs about falling such as, "Oh dear, I failed again. I am not a very good person. I had better not try again, or I might fall again, and then what would people think?"

When we rediscover that childlike quality of not thinking through a programmed thought system, our lives become as much fun as a child's. We lose all forms of insecurity, and each day is full of wonder, adventure, and delight in all there is to experience in life.

If it seems that I am going on and on about this principle, it is because I know this can be the most diffi-cult one to *understand.* Most people try to figure it out from their programmed thought system. The filters of the thought system created the distortions in the first place, so it is impossible to see things differently through that same perspective. Thus, I am saying the same thing over and over in different ways in hopes that one of the explanations will sneak past your filters and reach your inner wisdom, where all great discoveries and new learn-ing take place.

Looking at life through your programmed thought system is the same as looking at the world through

extremely dark glasses labeled "judgment," "blame," "expectations," "pride," "ego," "anger," "shoulds," and other forms of insecurity based on thought. These glasses are like blinders and filters that distort your view of life. The distortion becomes your reality and shuts out everything else, including the truth. Are you wondering, "What *is* the truth?"

The truth is what you see when you take off the dark glasses (dismiss negative thoughts) and access the wisdom of your heart. Have you ever noticed how different everything looks when you replace judgment with compassion, complaints with gratitude, hate with love? Whenever you have any negative feelings, you can recognize that you are wearing one of your pairs of dark glasses. As soon as you dismiss your thoughts, you will see from the perspective of your inner wisdom, and your reality will change.

Sometimes you may be aware that you are looking at the world through those dark glasses, but you can't seem to drop them because they feel stuck on with superglue. It may seem as if you are stuck in your thought system. Knowing what is happening, even when you can't seem to get out of it, shortens the "stuckness" tremendously. It is only thinking about your stuckness and taking it seriously, perhaps even obsessing about it, that allows it to hang on and get worse. It helps simply to realize what is happening and wait for it to pass rather than to worry about it. It might help to go for a walk, read a good book, meditate, or take a nap. This can be difficult to do if you take your thoughts with you. It is calming when you know you are waiting for the thoughts to pass.[6]

NOT A MATTER OF RIGHT OR WRONG

Understanding the principle of thought as a function does not imply there is a right or wrong way to think. Understanding the principle simply teaches you the many possibilities that come from thinking.

People who believe their thoughts are reality have forgotten the basic fact that they think and that they can think anything they want. They have forgotten (or perhaps never understood) that when they change their thoughts, their reality changes.

Sometimes it is very simple. If you don't like what you are thinking about, stop thinking about it.

---

6. Please see chapter 6 for more information on moods, and the importance of getting quiet while waiting for them to pass.

But, you may argue, how can I possibly stop thinking about what I'm thinking? I tried that, and it didn't work.

You keep thinking certain thoughts only when you believe they are reality and take them seriously. When you stop taking them seriously, it takes effort to keep thinking about them. *Understanding* the true nature of thinking makes it difficult to take any of your negative thoughts seriously.

When first learning about the principle of thinking as a function, many people find themselves in variations of the following states of thought.

STATES OF THOUGHT

1. Being caught up in thoughts and taking them seriously.

2. Being caught up in thoughts, but not taking them quite as seriously because of an understanding that they are just thoughts.

3. Being at rest. Dismissing thoughts and getting quiet to wait for inspiration and insight from inner wisdom.

4. Inspiration—when you are experiencing life from your heart or spiritual source.

You are usually in several variations of these states of thought throughout the day. Understanding the principles simply lets you know what is happening and thus frees you to live more of your life in the third and fourth states listed above.

In Wayne Dyer's *Gifts from Eykis*, Eykis points out, "Thinking is the basis for every single major and minor difficulty you encounter. The problems that arise in politics, religion, education, families, business, the military, society, medicine, and every form of human enterprise are due to self-programmed unreal thinking."[7]

When you understand your programmed thought system for the filter that it is, you will be able to bypass it, except for occasional, short visits. When you understand what happens when you are there, you won't want to stay for long. Each visit will simply confirm that thinking through your programmed thought system does not produce happiness and peace of mind (unless, of course, you are using it to remember useful facts and skills). Staying too long in states 1 or 2 may be letting you know that you have some healing to do.

SEEKING HELP

Sometimes your programmed thoughts and beliefs are so deeply embedded that they keep causing you problems—emotionally, physically, and spiritually. Dismissing your programmed thought system may give you temporary relief, but those subconscious beliefs keep returning and affecting your behavior and your health. You don't even know what thoughts you need to dismiss. They are beyond your conscious awareness. You are, however, profoundly aware of the misery they cause.

---

7. Wayne Dyer, *Gifts from Eykis* (New York: Pocket Books, 1983), pp. 118–119.

There is a wonderful story about a little girl who went to camp. During the day and evening, she was enthralled with all the activities, new friends, and storytelling around the bonfire. However, that evening a counselor found her crying in her bed. The counselor tried to comfort her in every way she could think of. Finally, she said, "God is always with you." The little girl said, "I know, but I want someone with skin on."

There are times when we all need a friend with skin on. Sometimes we need help from others who can comfort us or, when we are ready, show us another perspective.

We may need help from others to heal programmed thoughts and beliefs. Yes, beliefs can be healed, just as physical wounds can be healed. Positive thinking does not heal beliefs. Denial does not heal, and neither does repression. Beliefs are healed when the lie is exposed and understanding takes place. In her book *Heal the Cause*, Valerie Seeman Moreton writes, "When faulty programming is exposed and released, great relief is experienced. A light, open feeling of gratitude comes in and fills the empty space left by the old lie."[8]

When beliefs are healed, people don't have to *try* to give up the misconception that they are inadequate, unloved, or can't forgive. They couldn't hang on to those beliefs if they tried. Healing takes us immediately to our heart, where we feel love and compassion for self and others. We can't judge because we see the innocence of the people we believed had intentionally hurt us.

8. Valerie Seeman Moreton, N.D., *Heal the Cause* (San Diego: Kalos Publishing, 1996), p. 64.

Some find help that heals their beliefs by reading a book or talking with a friend. Others gain insights and inspiration in a church or a personal growth workshop. Others find help from therapy. No matter where you seek help, the criterion to look for is information or a process that helps you get beyond your programmed thought system and into your heart or spiritual source.

A wonderful part of healing is that we see the perfection of all things. Moreton puts it this way:

> Sometimes seeing the benefit of what has happened defuses deeply held emotions even further. Seeing the benefit of the situation creates a deeper understanding of how the universe is always working to support our highest good. . . . Acknowledging that benefit makes us more conscious of what is real and why forgiveness is always expedient. You can actually be happy about an uncomfortable experience when you see that a benefit has come from it. You can actually be grateful for it. Love and gratitude releases healing energy during a Process.[9]

Looking for the gift or life lesson in every situation is discussed more thoroughly in chapter 5.

THINKING IS NOT "THE BAD GUY"

At this point, or sooner, many people get the notion that thinking is "the bad guy" and that we should not think. Not at all. Thinking is a beautiful gift through which we experience the beauty of life. The key is understanding *where thoughts originate*. When they originate in your programmed thought system, you usually do not experi-

---

9. Moreton, pp. 269–270.

ence peace of mind and satisfaction. You experience serenity when thinking is the means you use to experience or express your inner wisdom, inspiration, and inherent good feelings that originate in your heart or from your spiritual source.

You are almost always thinking. *Understanding* helps you dismiss negative thoughts, which come from your programmed thought system, and to enjoy a nice life from your heart or spiritual source. *Understanding* helps you go from *here* (the misery of the thought system) to *serenity* (your natural state once the thought system is dismissed).

CHAPTER FIVE

The Principle of Feelings As a Compass

Your feelings are like a compass, letting you know where you are on the treasure map. Unconditional positive feelings let you know that you are experiencing life from your heart or spiritual source. When you feel bad emotionally, you are off course into your programmed thought system. Remember: It is impossible to have negative feelings without thoughts from your thought system. Thus, negative feelings act as a compass that lets you know that.

Just as Eskimos have many words to describe snow, we need many words to describe feelings. The feelings that come from our heart are very different from those that come from our programmed thought system. Heart feelings are unconditional, and they include a sense of peace, gratitude, love, and wisdom.

It is possible to have positive feelings from the thought system, but they are conditional and temporary.

Our tests show you're allergic to your negative thoughts.

For example, you may feel great if you win the lottery, until you discover that money doesn't buy happiness. You may feel good when you find your "true love," until you discover that many of those feelings were based on expectations and illusions from your thought system. True love is unconditional and everlasting.

When I was first learning about the principles, I believed that *understanding* meant I would never have

> When I understood that they were just thoughts, they could not hurt me.

negative feelings again, and I became very disappointed in myself whenever I took my thoughts seriously. By doing this, I had flipped out of my heart and into my head, where I used the information against myself. My feelings compass let me know this and that it was time to stop thinking about it and get quiet.

Before long, understanding led me back to my inner wisdom that let me know it didn't matter that my negative thoughts kept creeping in. (They were not actually "creeping" in. We become so proficient at instantaneously pulling up "files" from our programmed thought system that we forget they are still our moment-to-moment creations. It then seems that thoughts creep into our mind beyond our control, which is impossible.) After this realization, I experienced just "watching" those thoughts without judging them. I even felt a tolerant affection for my negative thoughts. I started seeing them as interesting or "humorous." When I understood that they were just thoughts, they could not hurt me. Most of the time, I could laugh and dismiss them. I have since learned that when it seems I can't dismiss them, they could be blessings in disguise—waiting for me to use them as opportunities for greater learning and healing.

All of us have subconscious beliefs based on decisions we made as children, formed from our perceptions at the time. Certain events may trigger emotional reactions from the past that are beyond our present awareness. Until we heal these *perception prisons*, thoughts and emotions do seem to "creep" in.

We all get off course into our thought system on a daily basis—some of us more often than others. An *understanding* of the four principles described in this book will help you avoid taking it seriously when you get off course, to avoid judging yourself, and to be open for the inspiration or healing that leads you back on course.

A word of caution: Many people claim they are just following their feelings compass when they do negative things, like "getting out" their anger or telling another person that their judgments about them are "the truth." This is a misuse of the feelings compass discussed in this chapter.

An *understanding* of this principle does not mean that you will never feel sad, hurt, or angry; it means that when you use these feelings as a compass, you will look to see where they are coming from—your thought system or your heart. Sometimes you may experience feelings from your heart or inner wisdom that *seem* similar to those from the thought system. While similar, they are totally different. As an example, I will paraphrase something I heard Wayne Dyer say in one of his lectures: "It angers and saddens me to see hunger in the world, but I know everything is in Divine Order. It is perfect that there is hunger in the world, and it is perfect that I want to do something about it." Instead of ranting and raving about the injustice of hunger, Wayne contributes regularly to the World Hunger Fund and does everything he can to raise the world consciousness to a level where hunger could not take place.

Other so-called negative feelings may come from the heart, but the outcome will be different. You may feel very sad when you lose a loved one. However, along with the sadness will be gratitude for the time spent with that loved one and an understanding of the perfection of all things. You will allow the sadness to teach you—perhaps to slow down and enjoy other loved ones in your life or to honor that loved one by living life to the fullest.

Too many people experience loss only from their thought system, which then becomes a hellish prison. Parents who have lost a child go into depression and totally neglect their living children. Spouses who have been abandoned live the rest of their lives in anger, bitterness, or seeking revenge. They could not do this if they understood the power of their thought systems and dismissed them so they would have access to the wisdom of their hearts.

THE ORIGIN OF FEELINGS

Unconditional good feelings and actions flow naturally from your heart. The feeling comes first and is then experienced through the function of your thinking. Negative feelings are experienced after you create negative thoughts from your thought system. In other words, if the feeling comes first, it is from your heart; if the feeling comes second, it is from your thought system.[1] For example, you see a newborn baby, and your heart is filled with wonder. The feeling of wonder comes first and then is processed through your function of thinking. On the other hand, you may have fearful thoughts about negative conditions in the world. You see a newborn baby and feel sad because of what this poor child will have to live through. The thoughts come first and affect your feelings.

---

1. Again, I wish we had more words to describe feelings. A feeling that is triggered from the subconscious may seem to come first, but it is not an "in the moment" feeling. It is a feeling based on subconscious thoughts from the past.

Soon after learning this, I had an experience that illustrates how thoughts can affect feelings. During a one-week seminar in which I was learning about the principles, I called home to see how my children were doing. I was informed that my thirteen-year-old son had been suspended from school.

This is how he told the story: "I found some cigarettes in my locker. I don't know how they got there. I was just putting them in my pocket to take them to the principal when a teacher came by and took me to the principal."

It felt as though my thoughts went crazy for a few minutes (but actually I created crazy thoughts): "He is lying to us. I'm a failure as a mother. If he's smoking cigarettes, he's probably also using alcohol and drugs. He is going to ruin his life. What will people think?" I was very upset, so my feelings compass let me know loud and clear that I was caught up in my thought system and was not seeing clearly. I dismissed my feelings compass instead of my thoughts for a minute and used more thoughts to bury my inner wisdom: "Yes, but this is different. These are really terrible circumstances over which I have no control. How could I possibly see them differently? I am going to have to scold him severely, ground him for at least a month, take away all his privileges, and let him know he is ruining his life." Fortunately, I had too much faith in the principles to take those thoughts seriously for long, and inspiration quickly surfaced. I then saw the circumstances in a completely different way and felt understanding and compassion for my son's view of the situation. He had just entered junior high school, where the pressure is enormous to follow the crowd rather than to follow common sense.

When I got home, I listened to my inspiration and knew what to do. I sat down with my son, put my arm around him, and said, "I'll bet it's tough trying to figure out how to say no to your friends so you won't be called a nerd or a party pooper." He had been expecting my usual craziness and hardly knew how to respond to my sanity.

He said tentatively, "Yeah."

I went on, "And I'll bet the only reason you would ever lie to us is because you love us so much you don't want to disappoint us." Tears filled his eyes, and he gave me a big hug. With tears in my own eyes, I reassured him, "If you think you could ever disappoint us enough to diminish our love, then we are not doing a good enough job of letting you know how much we love you, unconditionally."

> Whenever I feel upset, angry, judgmental, disappointed, or any other negative emotion, I know that my feelings are being created by thoughts I am taking seriously. As soon as I recognize that and dismiss the thoughts, I am filled with my inherent good feelings.

We can only guess what the results would have been had I followed my crazy thoughts to interact with my son. My guess is that my craziness would have inspired increased rebelliousness instead of increased closeness. No matter what the results, my inner wisdom lets me know that he has a right to live his own life and learn his own lessons. I know he will have a much better chance to experience his inner wisdom if he feels unconditional love from me instead of my ego's need to judge him.

I am continually grateful for the principle of using my feelings as a compass to let me know when I am "off track." Whenever I feel upset, angry, judgmental, disappointed, or any other negative emotion, I know that my feelings are being created by thoughts I am taking seriously. As soon as I recognize that and dismiss the thoughts, I am filled with my inherent good feelings.

Dismissing negative thoughts is not the same as sticking your head in the sand. It is more like taking off blinders and filters so that you can see the situation with perspective. Sometimes the problem disappears along with the negative thoughts. Other times the problem may still be there, but you are able to view it differently. You will see solutions rather than problems because from your inner wisdom solutions are clear.

The chart on the following page has helped many people use their feelings compass to increase their *understanding*. It is a graphic representation of the feelings and conditions we experience from our heart and those we experience when thinking from our programmed thought system.

Try adding other words to the columns on the chart. A word such as *responsibility* feels like duty or compulsion when added to the thought-system column. Responsibility feels natural and easy when added to the heart column. Notice how different *sex* feels in either column, or *charity, strength, giving, discipline, teaching, control, desire,* or any other concept you can think of.

Even so-called positive attributes can come from the thought system instead of the heart. *Admiration* is an example. Put that word in each column and see how the meaning

✿ FEELINGS COMPASS CHART

Heart or Spiritual Source	Programmed Thought System
High level of consciousness	*Low level of consciousness*
Security	Insecurity
Love	Expectations
Serenity and happiness	Stress and coping
Joyful productivity	Stressful productivity
Compassion	Judgments
Contentment	Wanting more, better, different
Wisdom	Rules ("shoulds" and "shouldn'ts")
Forgiveness	Blame, anger, self-righteousness
Gratitude	Blindness to miracles
Inspiration	Beliefs
Peace of mind (Serenity)	Depression and/or anxiety
The beauty of now	Past-or future-oriented
Natural positive feelings	Positive thinking

changes. Is your admiration based on your perception that a person has met your expectations, done the "right thing," or done a good job of proving his ego? Or is admiration based on unconditional love and gratitude? Can you admire a person as you would a flower or a sunset?

Also notice what happens when you take some of the words from the heart column and add them to the thought-system column. Love and forgiveness, for example, do not have the same feeling when shifted. How many of us have experienced the contamination of love when we add expectations and judgments? How many of us have felt self-righteous for forgiving?

Again, I want to clarify that I'm not saying any of this is wrong. *Understanding* the principles gives us a road map to where we are; it doesn't tell us where we *should* be. I have already mentioned that there are gifts to be found and lessons to be learned from the experiences that come through your thought system. Of course, as soon as you see this, you have returned to your heart or spiritual source.

We all go in and out of these states of mind every day, depending on what thoughts we are thinking. Remembering that thinking is an ability makes it natural to quit taking our thoughts seriously and to leave room for heart messages. These messages will immediately change our states of mind and our feelings. Mental illness or mental health is simply a moment-to-moment state of mind. Mental illness and unhappiness are states that occur when we forget that thinking is a function.

POSITIVE THINKING

Did you wonder why positive thinking was in the column on the right? The feelings and wisdom you experience from your heart or spiritual source are different from what you experience through positive thinking. Positive thinkers forget that they have the ability to think and try to change thoughts instead of dismissing them and allowing wisdom to surface naturally. They assume that thoughts "happen" to them and that, through positive thinking, they can control which thoughts happen or can change the ones that have already happened.

They are dealing with thinking as a reality rather than as a function.

When you are enjoying a beautiful sunset or feeling love, wouldn't it be ridiculous to stop and say, "I'd better start thinking positively about this"? Even to have the *thought* of positive thinking means that you are having negative thoughts, which you think you "should" change. No "shoulds" are involved when you are in your heart—just natural, positive feelings or wisdom and obvious things to do to experience positive results in your life and relationships. The battleground is eliminated. If you are experiencing a battle in your mind, you are operating from your thought system, not from your heart.

Positive thinking is also conditional: "I will be happy if I have positive thoughts" or "I'm a success when I think positively and a failure when I don't." It is true that you will be happy if you have positive thoughts, but when positive thoughts come from your heart, they are natural and effortless. Have you ever wanted to think positively but felt like a failure because you couldn't? Perhaps what you are learning now will help you understand why it seems to work sometimes and not others.

Annie experienced a failure of positive thinking after a fight with her brother. She went into her room and tried to forget about it by thinking of enjoyable things. First she thought about baseball, but that didn't work because she just wanted to hit her brother with a bat. Then she tried thinking about soccer but felt like kicking her brother instead of the ball.

When Annie realized that no kind of thinking helped, she stopped thinking and started looking out the

window. She quietly watched the birds and enjoyed looking at the trees and flowers, and soon, instead of thinking
positively or negatively about the past, she became engrossed in the present. Before long, Annie felt good
again. She apologized to her brother and spent the rest of
the afternoon playing with him.

Positive thinking comes from your programmed
thought system and takes effort. Positive thinking is not
necessary when you use your thinking ability for the natural expression of beautiful feelings, which come through
your heart in all the positive forms, such as inspiration,
gratitude, and unconditional love.

When you are experiencing any stress or unhappiness in your life, it may help to take a look at the Feelings
Compass Chart. Use your feelings compass. Allow your
inner wisdom to let you know what thoughts or beliefs
from the column on the right are causing your misery. As
soon as you "see" it, that *understanding* may allow you to
drop those thoughts and access your heart.

It is amazing how different you will feel when you
see the world from your heart or spiritual source. Love,
joy, compassion, and wisdom flow.

CHAPTER SIX

The Principle
of Separate Realities

Another well-kept secret is the fact that everyone lives in a separate reality. This simply means that we all interpret things differently and that each of us views the world from his or her own private logic. A popular example often used to explain the principle of separate realities is that everyone who sees an accident describes it differently. The reason becomes obvious when we understand that everyone sees through the filters of his or her own unique, programmed thought system.

We have separate realities because everyone has personal memories, interpretations, and beliefs that act like filters through which present events are seen. When we view the world through these filters, it is impossible to see what *is* with fresh perspective.

Again, you may object, "Everyone knows that." It is true that most of us have heard this principle, but we

forget to apply it in our lives. Hearing about separate realities and *understanding* the principle at a deep level are
not the same. When we really understand the fact of separate realities, we will stop spending so much time and
energy trying to change the reality of others. Remember,
there is a difference between understanding from an intellectual level (from our heads) and understanding from
insight (from our hearts). When we forget about separate
realities, we seem to take everything personally. When
someone says something hurtful, we get our feelings
hurt. With an understanding of separate realities, we
would feel compassion instead. After all, what anyone
says is about them, not about anyone else. Doesn't it
make more sense to feel compassion for the person who

sees the world through negative filters than to accept what they say as reality?

Without *understanding*, we are unaware of our filters, and we therefore think our interpretations are real. We become convinced that if we try hard enough, we can persuade others that our reality is the right one. This *never works*—so marriages may break up in hostility, parents and children experience "generation gaps," and nations go to war. The reverse can also apply. Some people think their reality is wrong or is not as good as other people's, and so they may spend a lot of time feeling inadequate, insecure, and depressed.

When you don't understand separate realities, you might wonder, "How could they possibly be like that or do that? They would be happier if they did it my way, liked my kind of music (especially at the volume I prefer), ate the foods I like, and loaded the dishwasher the way I do." These thoughts and judgments can create a great deal of misery in the form of anger or other stressful emotions.

I had an opportunity to learn this *again* when I became very upset with one of my children. The details aren't as important as the lesson. I knew I was deeply stuck in my thought system, and I couldn't seem to drop it. I kept wondering, "How could he do that? He is making a huge mistake." I couldn't understand how he could justify his behavior.

Finally, I sat down to meditate and ask for messages from my heart, which came almost immediately. The first was, *You wonder how he could have done such a thing. How many times in your life have you done things that would invite the same question from others? How many huge mistakes have you made? It is his life to live.*

I don't mean that I heard a voice, exactly. This is simply an example of the kind of wisdom that is expressed in thoughts that come from our hearts or spiritual sources instead of our programmed thought systems. The message seemed so obvious once I "heard" it, but I couldn't hear it while stuck in the perception prison of my thought system.

> When we truly *understand* the principle of separate realities, we see differences with a more compassionate interest.

This story also provides an example of the mirror insight process (described in chapter 8). Often, whatever we find annoying in someone else is really a reflection of an area where we need some work ourselves. We often don't want to see this, especially when we think that what the other person does is so much worse than what we do. With *understanding*, we can see the humor in this. If what we do is less serious, how much better our time could be spent correcting our own foibles than judging others. As I have said before, a message from your heart often seems humorous when you finally *see* it.

Other messages from my inner wisdom followed: *Look at the trouble you create for yourself when you think others should live up to your expectations or do "what is right" and "for their own good" according to you.*

I had to laugh at my self-righteousness when I *saw* it. I had believed that my son's actions had made me miserable; instead, I remembered that *my thoughts about what he did* made me miserable. I felt gratitude for the lesson and compassion for my son—and for my parents who often made themselves miserable over my actions and mistakes.

When we truly *understand* the principle of separate realities, we see differences with a more compassionate interest. We may prefer not to spend time with some people whose reality creates negative energy. This choice, however, will be made with compassion for them and respect for ourselves rather than with negative judgments and self-righteousness.

Visitors usually respect separate realities when visiting another country; they certainly wouldn't be welcome if they told people of other countries that they should speak their language and change their customs. Traveling is enjoyable when visitors learn about different cultures and traditions and respect differences. Wouldn't it be wonderful if we approached personal relationships with the same wonder and respect?

Phil and Lisa experienced separate realities soon after they were married. Phil was an "early bird"; he loved getting up at dawn full of energy and ready to enjoy the day. Every morning he bounded out of bed and sang loudly in the shower, hoping Lisa would wake up.

Noticing her still in bed with the covers pulled over her head, he would noisily bounce on the bed as he put on his shoes and socks, thinking, "If she really loved me, she would get up and enjoy this time with me."

Lisa, totally annoyed at what she saw as his "inconsiderateness," would be thinking, "If he really loved me,

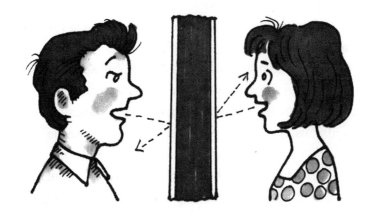

he would know I hate getting up early and would be quiet and let me sleep."

They often discussed their differences, but neither really "heard" the other because each was more interested in changing than understanding the other. Both felt as though they were talking to a wall as they tried to make their points. What they did not realize is that they were talking to two walls—the wall of their own reality and the wall of the other's reality.

Christmases were a disaster. When Lisa was growing up, everyone in her family had received one very nice, expensive present for Christmas. In Phil's family everyone had enjoyed the fun of opening several inexpensive presents. So Lisa would buy Phil one nice, expensive present, and Phil would buy Lisa several inexpensive presents. Every Christmas they felt disappointed and misunderstood, each thinking that the other was too dense to know how to really enjoy Christmas.

We may be amused at Phil and Lisa for not seeing how simply they could solve their problems by respecting their separate realities instead of by trying to change each other. Nonetheless, when dealing with our own precious beliefs, we are often just as blind.

Have you noticed how important it seems to tell others, especially those you love, when you think they are wrong? Then you wonder why they don't appreciate it.

Bill used to dread visiting his father because they both always ended up with bad feelings. Bill said, "We used to spend all our time together arguing about who was right and who was wrong. I was certainly never going to admit I was wrong because it seemed very clear to me that I wasn't. Dad would not admit he was wrong, even though I made every effort to let him know how old-fashioned his ideas were. *Understanding* separate realities was a godsend for me. Dad and I no longer argue over our differences. I respect how he sees things and know I would see them the same way if I were in his shoes. Now we just share the love and gratitude we have and enjoy each other's company."

Nor is it helpful to judge your own reality. One day when I was judging myself for not having a deeper under-standing of the principles, I suddenly realized that any form of judgment would only block my *understanding*. When I stopped judging my present reality, I could see that to say I should be farther along than I am, or that someone else should have a different reality than they do, makes as much sense as saying a rosebud should be a rose in full bloom.

Every human being is in the process of evolving, learning, and growing (or refusing to change). Getting in the way with our judgments only creates negativity and impedes progress. Can you imagine how much more helpful we would be to ourselves and others if we were loving and compassionate instead of judgmental?

A master gardener does not fret because her roses are not growing into petunias; rather she simply nurtures all of the flowers with water, weeding, and fertilizer so that they can reach their full potential as roses, petunias, or whatever they are. We can likewise simply enjoy and nurture who we and others are.

> When we quit seeing separate realities as right or wrong, we see ourselves and others without judgment, and we are free from the negative feelings that cloud our vision when we are judgmental.

"Shoulds" are not necessary when we have access to our inherent good feelings. Nurturing ourselves and others comes naturally from the heart. Our inner wisdom lets us know that the key is to love and nurture, not to judge.

Some people have put this information into their thought system and misused it. I have heard people say in a disparaging tone of voice, "Well, that is just your separate reality, and I have a right to mine." This was not said from love, compassion, and respect. The principles (when truly understood) can never be used against others—or ourselves.

Our world expands greatly when we understand and appreciate separate realities. It is possible to enjoy differences (or at least understand them) instead of fighting over them. When we quit seeing separate realities as right or wrong, we see ourselves and others without judgment, and we are free from the negative feelings that cloud our vision when we are judgmental. People who insist that they must be judgmental to keep the world from "going to hell" put themselves in a state of mental hell, which does not help the world. Love energy helps the world. If you cannot find it in your heart to love a negative person, at least love yourself enough to stay out of his or her way, without judgment.

If your programmed thought system is resisting, you are probably dredging up the worst possible examples you can imagine, such as murder, rape, and burglary—or a spouse who did some terrible thing. Self-righteousness, hatred, or any form of negative judgment only keeps you separated from your heart and inner wisdom that could lead you to positive action. You then become like the thing or person you judge or hate, spreading more negativity in the world. When you live from your heart, you will know what to do about these issues to get the best possible results. You will act from love and wisdom.

You may argue, "But some things really are wrong!" With understanding, we see that this need not be an issue because everyone does the best that he can with what he knows. When we see the innocence in all behaviors and feel compassion or interest, instead of judgment, we are much happier. We can't help anyone else when we are unhappy. And when we have understanding, it is natural to "forgive them, for they know not what they do." However, *we* will know what to do. It is natural to follow the Serenity Prayer when we wish to experience life from our spiritual source:

God, grant me the serenity to accept the things I cannot change, the courage to change the things I can, and the wisdom to know the difference.

All relationships can be enhanced through an *understanding* of the principle of separate realities. It is often said that many people would rather be *right* than be loved. In the thought system, this seems to be the case.

I recently had the opportunity to recognize that I was choosing to be "right" instead of choosing love. My husband and I were getting ready to come home from a large convention. He wanted to get in line for the hotel shuttle to the airport two hours early. I wanted to get in line one hour early. We were both getting annoyed at what we perceived to be obtuse behavior in the other. Each of us thought the reality of the other was ridiculous.

My feelings compass gave me a wake-up call, and I consciously chose to go into my heart. From that space, I said to Barry, "I wonder what would happen if we looked at this differently and had compassion for what it would cost either of us to follow the lead of the other. The price I would have to pay to go early is the discomfort of spending more time at the airport. The price you would have to pay is worry and anxiety about being late."

It was obvious to me that it would be easier for me to change than for him—because I had moved into my heart. From my heart, I saw his separate reality as endearing instead of wrong. I also saw the benefits of getting to the airport in plenty of time to relax. I saw how I could learn from him when I quit seeing his point of view as ridiculous.

Some people could see this as a technique—but the key was moving out of my head and into my heart where everything looked and felt different. It was contagious. Barry felt loved and responded by moving into his heart. He said, "Well, I guess I do exaggerate." We laughed, left for the airport early, and had a good time being together.

Being loving and loved is much nicer than being "right." In the heart, where separate realities are seen with interest and compassion, loving has top priority.

CHAPTER SEVEN

The Principle of Mood Levels, or Levels of Consciousness

Everyone has moods. Some people seem to fluctuate between extremes more than others, but we all experience times when we feel good and times when we feel low. Have you noticed how different your own separate reality is, depending on whether you're feeling high or low? In different moods, it is possible to see the same things differently. For example, recall the last time you were driving along in a good mood and someone needed to cut in front of you, and you cheerfully waved them in, remembering how often you have been in the same situation. Now, think of another time when you were in a low mood and you stepped on the gas, determined not to let them in, mumbling about how stupid and inconsiderate *they* were. When you are in a low mood, everything looks

bad. You may feel overwhelmed and have feelings of impending doom. There seems to be no way out.

> A quiet mind is the best cure for a low mood.

A higher mood or level of consciousness simply means that you can see things with more perspective and with greater *understanding* from your heart or spiritual source. Lower moods or levels of consciousness simply mean that you have lost perspective and understanding because you are living in your programmed thought system.

Reality is greatly distorted with lost perspective. The distortion is heavily sprinkled with ego, expectations, and judgments—all characteristics of the thought system. At a time of lost perspective, however, your distorted thoughts seem like the only possibility. I'm sure you have experienced both high and low moods or levels of consciousness, and you are aware of how differently you function during each state of mind. Since high moods or levels of consciousness are obviously so much better, and you have experienced that state of mind many times, you may wonder why you can't stay there all the time.

Sometimes low moods just happen as part of our physiological functioning. Research in biorhythms has shown that we experience intellectual, emotional, and physical cycles that peak and ebb. When low moods are physiological, it makes sense to simply wait for them to pass. Usually, however, a belief or thought is the culprit. Often you are unaware of the thoughts that have created your low moods. Trying to figure out the cause usually makes things worse because you are trying to figure it out from the very thought system that created the low mood. The secret is knowing that moods are not nearly as bad as the thoughts you have about them. Thus, the solution for low moods or levels of consciousness that are caused by thoughts is the same as those caused by physiology: The key is to patiently wait for the mood to pass. Sometimes you don't have to wait long because an understanding of the source often leads to the immediate dismissal of your thought system followed by wisdom from your heart. When neither patience nor insight is effective, you might need the help of "someone with skin on."

I remember when I used to get depressed. Feeling inadequate and insecure about something, I would retreat into depression. Then I would be upset with myself for being depressed, thereby feeling more inadequate and insecure. How depressing! I did not understand the vicious cycle I was creating with my thoughts. Later, I started looking forward to my depressions because I used them as an excuse to lie in bed all day and read. My depressions quit lasting very long when I started enjoying them. I finally saw the obvious and realized that I did not have to get depressed in order to take a day to rest and enjoy myself. I could simply follow my inner wisdom, which was letting me know it was time to get quiet.

> The moment we understand that we are seeing things from a lower level of consciousness, we have jumped to a higher level of con- sciousness. It takes understanding to realize when we are not seeing something with understanding.

A quiet mind is the best cure for a low mood. You have a quiet mind naturally when you dismiss thoughts from your programmed thought system. Sometimes the simple realization that "it is only a mood" will be enough to immediately raise your level of consciousness. The moment this happens, your thoughts will be dis- missed, and you will have ac- cess to your heart, which will allow you to see things from a higher perspective. Your reality will change.

Ellen was upset because a department store had failed to refund her money as promised. She took out her anger on the customer service clerk, who talked back rudely to Ellen. As soon as Ellen realized what was hap- pening, her mood shifted and she saw things differently. She then said to the clerk, "You really have a tough job, don't you?"

The clerk responded immediately, in a better mood, "I sure do." From then on, she was very helpful, and the problem was resolved.

It all goes back to thought. In lower levels of consciousness, we react from a thought system full of troublesome beliefs and judgments. In higher levels of consciousness, it is natural to see things with love, joy, gratitude, or simple interest. When action needs to be taken, we know what to do to increase love instead of fear.

It is impossible to see anything with *understanding* when we are in a low mood. It makes no sense to trust our thoughts or feelings when we are in a low level of consciousness because they are being filtered through our programmed thought system rather than coming from wisdom and common sense. Understanding this principle teaches us to get quiet (verbally, physically, and mentally) and wait for the low mood to pass.

Don't underestimate the power of quiet to help you let go of troublesome thoughts and move into your heart. Be gentle with yourself. It may take several days or weeks. Looking for the life lesson or benefit of your situation may help. If you think that another person has contributed to your low mood, looking in "the mirror" might help—when you see your reflection with insight, humor, and compassion. Prolonged low moods may be letting you know that you have some out-of-awareness thoughts and beliefs that need healing. When you can't seem to access your own inner wisdom, it is fine to seek the help of someone who has access to theirs. I would not suggest seeking help from anyone who does not understand the importance of leading you out of your programmed thought system and into your inner wisdom.

NOW YOU SEE IT, NOW YOU DON'T

High or low moods (or levels of consciousness) are not a matter for value or moral judgment. Consciousness is a state of awareness, perspective, or insight. Sometimes we see it (*understand*), and sometimes we don't. The moment we *understand* that we are seeing things from a lower level of consciousness, we have jumped to a higher level of consciousness. It takes *understanding* to realize when we are not seeing something with understanding. So, the moment we recognize we have not been *seeing* clearly, we are seeing that much more clearly. However, if in the next moment we judge ourselves because we didn't see clearly initially, we lose our understanding again. Be gentle with yourself.

When we are in a good mood or higher level of consciousness, we feel love, compassion, forgiveness, and gratitude. We feel satisfaction and peace of mind. We see things with greater understanding and perspective. We do not have to try to make ourselves feel these things through positive thinking; in a higher level of consciousness, we feel them naturally.

You may ask, "What about all those times when I am not in a good mood or at a higher level of consciousness? How do I get out of my low mood if I don't try to figure it out or use positive thinking?" This question indicates that you are having a difficult time understanding this principle because of the filters of your thought system and the inadequacy of words to get through to your heart. Perhaps the following example will help.

Feeling low happens, just as storms happen. We don't try to figure out how to stop a storm, or why it is there, or how to change it. We simply do whatever is necessary to minimize damage, make ourselves as comfortable as possible, and wait for the storm to pass.

A sailor knows the importance of dropping the sails when coming into a storm. With understanding, we know the importance of dropping the thought system when we are in a low mood or have any negative feelings.

Low moods can change immediately with recognition, or, like the flu, they may hang around even when we know what they are. When we get the flu, we know that the best thing to do is to take care of ourselves until it passes; we are also careful not to spread it around. It is wise to treat your low moods in the same way.

> It is difficult to hang on to silly thoughts while appreciating all there is to be grateful for.

Understanding the principle of mood levels helps you to know how effective it is to get quiet and wait for low moods to pass—or to know enough not to spread your bad moods around—or to forgive yourself and others when you don't have enough understanding to snap out of it or wait for it to pass. There are many levels of understanding.

Some people suppose that there is only one level of understanding and that once you have it you will never lose it again. This has not been my experience, however, nor has it been the experience of anyone I know. An understanding of math principles doesn't mean that we will never make a mistake in addition. However, math principles will help us find the mistake and correct it.

It now seems perfect to me that I get lost in my programmed thought system once in a while. I can find so many gifts in the experience. Of course, while I'm lost, it is impossible to see the gifts. It is not helpful to beat up on myself. *It is helpful to know that it is normal, and that I can't see it until I see it.* Using the principles can help me and you understand what happened and how to find our way back to understanding, where we see the gifts and feel gratitude.

GRATITUDE

I have found that one of the quickest ways to change my mood is through gratitude. It is difficult to hang on to silly thoughts while appreciating all there is to be grateful for. Once I was in such a sour mood, I couldn't think of anything to be grateful for. Then I looked down at my hands and was struck by the absolute miracle of my ability to move my fingers. Then I looked up and saw the sky. How beautiful! Love, beauty, and miracles are all around us whenever we are willing to notice. When we are stuck in our thought system, we miss so much. We could be walking on a spectacular beach or through a beautiful forest and miss all the beauty if our focus is on troublesome thoughts—just as we miss simple pleasures and the joy of personal relationships, which don't require spectacular settings.

Sue Pettit had a wonderful insight about moods and thoughts and was inspired to write a poem entitled "Lily's

Loose."[1] Notice the similarity of Lily Tomlin's role as Ernestine at the switchboard from the old TV show *Laugh-In* and what happens when we let our thought system take over.

Lily's Loose

Lily is the operator at the switchboard of my brain.
And when she starts reacting, my life becomes insane.
She's supposed to be employed by me—and play a passive role.
But anytime I'm insecure—Lily takes control.

Lily's loose, Lily's loose, Lily's loose today.
Tell everyone around me just to clear out of my way.
The things I say won't make much sense—all COMMON SENSE is lost.
'Cause when Lily's at the switchboard—my wires all get crossed.

Lily is my own creation, thought I needed her with me
To organize and then recall all my life's history.
But she started taking liberty with all my information.
And whenever she starts plugging in—I get a bad sensation.

Lily's loose, Lily's loose, Lily's loose today.
Tell all my friends and relatives to clear out of my way.
I don't give hugs and kisses when I'm in this frame of mind.
And please don't take me seriously—it'd be a waste of time.

She looks out through my eyeballs and sees what I do see.

---

1. "Lily's Loose" and many other wonderful poems, which beautifully and humorously illustrate the principles of Psychology of Mind, are available in a book entitled *Coming Home* by Sue Pettit, available through HOPE by calling 1-605-226-3326.

Then hooks up wires to my past—she thinks she's helping me!
When I'm in a good mood, I can smile at her endeavor.
But when I'm in a bad mood—Lily's boss, and is she clever.

Lily's loose, Lily's loose, Lily's loose today.
Tell the world to hurry by and stay out of my way.
I'm feeling very scattered—I'm lost in my emotion.
Lily's on a rampage, and she's causing a commotion.

I heard a wonderful story from a lady in Connecticut who said that she read this poem to her teenage son. Then, every time she would start lecturing or scolding, one of them would see what was happening and say, "Lily's Loose," and both would start laughing.

LAUGHTER

Laughter has the power to transform moods. Have you ever noticed that as soon as you can laugh at or about something, you see it differently? With *understanding*, it is difficult to take things too seriously. The seriousness is usually based on thoughts and beliefs from the thought system that incorporate judgments, "shoulds," and "shouldn'ts." Most of the issues we take so seriously create stress instead of serenity, such as the need for control. Control issues can seem particularly funny when seen with perspective.

I had an interesting insight about control while on a ski hill. I was snowplowing so that I would have more control. It was a lot of work—and not much fun. Then I looked up the hill and saw the expert skiers. They were not snowplowing or demonstrating any other kind of "controlling behavior," yet they seemed to have perfect control—and were having lots of fun. I realized that their control came from a mastery of skiing techniques and principles, not from behavior that provided an illusionary sense of control.

I applied this insight to relationships between teachers and students, parents and children, and husbands and wives. When we stop our controlling behavior (which comes from fear and insecurity) and apply principles of love, dignity and respect, control doesn't seem to be an issue. We naturally have control without acting controlling. We don't try to make people change, yet we are often inspired to do things that may invite change. The inspiration we receive often includes humor.

In our parenting workshops, we suggest that parents quit taking many things seriously and adopt an "isn't it cute" attitude around some things that upset them. I was driving myself crazy over the fact that my teenagers kept leaving empty cereal bowls in their rooms. Not only could I never find a cereal bowl when I needed one, but the bowls in their rooms were caked with dried cereal and sour milk. I ranted and raved until I used my feelings compass to realize that I was obviously coming from my thought system. As soon as I dismissed my judgments, I really could see it as a cute, teenage phenomenon. Then I was inspired to take action from love and humor. We discussed the "problem" at a family meeting. After laughing about how normal it is for teenagers to do things like this, we came up with a solution. Every other week I would collect their cereal bowls every day as a reminder to myself of how much I love them. Every other week they would bring their cereal bowls to the dishwasher out of love for me. Since I know how easy it is for teenagers to get distracted from things that are a priority to adults, we agreed that it would be fine for me to put a love note on their pillows when they forgot. This worked much better than all the ranting and raving—and was a lot more fun.

Nothing I did about the cereal bowls from my thought system was effective. Those actions created rebellion, anger, and frustration. None of us felt loved. What I did from my heart created love and harmony— and a solution that was effective.

HELPING OTHERS IN A LOW MOOD

So-called techniques feel very different when coming from your heart than when coming from your thought system. The technique of *reflective listening* provides a good example. Reflective listening simply means to validate what a person is saying by reflecting the words back. If you do this from your thought system, it is likely that you will sound like a parrot. If you do reflective listening from your heart, you will reflect feelings, as well as the spoken words, out of compassion. You won't take the words of others so seriously because you'll know that they are coming from a low mood or from beliefs from the programmed thought system. Their words are often a "cover up" for deeper feelings. People you are listening to don't need "advice" from your thought system. They need compassion from your heart, as in the following example.

Sally was very angry at her sister because of an argument that had taken place two years ago. The sister wanted to come for a visit, but Sally refused to see her. Her husband, Joel, gave her some "spiritual" advice. "Don't you think it is time to let go of your anger and learn to forgive? Don't you know how much this anger is hurting you?"

Sally did not find the "advice" helpful. She felt hurt, and told Joel, "You just don't understand."

Joel shared what had happened with a friend who had an understanding of the four principles. She asked Joel, "What do you think would happen if you stopped seeing the details of what she is saying and instead saw her as a person who is caught up in her thought system and is in a very low mood? Try giving her compassion through reflective listening instead of advice."

That night, Joel apologized to Sally for giving her advice and said, "I can understand how hurt you felt by the argument with your sister."

Sally responded defensively, "It seems like every time I try to get close to her, she says something mean to me."

Joel said, "Sounds like you are feeling scared that she might hurt you again. Staying away is a good way to protect yourself from that."

Sally started to cry. She felt so validated. She hadn't known herself that that was what she was doing, but she realized that it was true when Joel said it with such loving compassion. Feeling his love put her into her heart (and a higher level of consciousness), where she started to feel compassion for her sister and herself. "Donna is critical just like my mother was. We both do that. We hated it when our mother did it, but we now do the same thing."

Joel said, "Sounds like you are understanding that she may be scared, too, and doesn't know how to break those old patterns."

Sally said, "I hadn't really thought of it before, but maybe we could talk about it and help each other. We could remind each other when we notice we are doing old stuff and jokingly say, 'Knock it off.' I really don't want to repeat those old patterns. My mom didn't know any better, but maybe we can learn."

In this example, Joel helped Sally find her own solutions by avoiding advice. This often happens when someone feels compassion from another. It is difficult to stay in a low mood when feeling loved, and from a higher mood we have access to our own inner wisdom.

Other people may not find their own solutions. That is not the point. The point is that people can't hear advice from others or their own inner wisdom when they are feeling discouraged. Compassion does not have ulterior motives. People need our compassion even if they stay in a low mood.

Use your feelings compass to recognize a low mood—in yourself and others. This will often transport you immediately out of your low mood and into your heart, where you will see and do things from love and inspiration—for yourself and others.

CHAPTER EIGHT

The Struggle Can Lead to Understanding

Some people experience a mental struggle when they first hear these principles. Because they habitually use their thought systems to try to figure things out, they can't imagine solving problems any other way. Further, they are used to blaming circumstances for causing their feelings and are unaccustomed to seeing that it is their way of *thinking about circumstances* that creates their feelings.

Others misinterpret the principles to mean that they should quit thinking and become a blob. The opposite is true. Once you truly *understand* the principles, you stop being a slave to your thought system, and thinking as a function becomes your servant. When you are a slave to your thought system, you lack access to the inner wisdom of your heart or spiritual source, thus restricting your perspective and awareness of unlimited possibilities.

Humans rarely stop thinking, even in their sleep. The point is not to stop thinking but to understand that *thinking is a function* because that understanding helps you dismiss troublesome thoughts, and to use your thinking ability to experience the wonders that come to you from your heart or spiritual source.

Understanding frees you from the prison of your programmed thought system. And yet, a misunderstanding of the principles can lead to increased programming and misuse. I often heard comments like the following while attending seminars to learn about the principles of Psychology of Mind:

> You can appreciate your mistakes when you realize that they are simply part of your learning experience. You can enjoy being a rosebud until you become a rose in full bloom.

"I'm afraid to ask a question, or people will know I'm coming from my thought system instead of a higher level of consciousness."

"I still have negative thoughts, so I must not *understand* anything."

"I'm a failure because I yelled at my children. I lost my patience and forgot to come from my heart to see the insecurity behind their behavior."

"I really thought I understood and would not get caught up in my thought system again. The very next day I let myself get hooked into negativity, just like Pavlov's dog. I felt very discouraged and disappointed in myself."

"I just can't feel compassion when my wife drinks, or my husband yells at me, or a friend disappoints me, or things don't turn out the way I want them to. I get angry or upset."

These comments indicate a lack of deeper *understanding*, but it is not helpful to add negative judgment. We do the best we can based on our level of understanding, and we make mistakes on our way to deeper understanding. This is normal. When we first learned math principles, we made mistakes. As our understanding grows, we make fewer mistakes or use our understanding to correct the mistakes. *Negative judgment only hampers the inspiration that encourages learning.* You can appreciate your mistakes when you realize that they are simply part of your learning experience. You can enjoy being a rosebud until you become a rose in full bloom.

With *understanding*, the concepts of "perfect" and "mistakes" are totally different. Whenever you get upset about mistakes or "not being perfect," you are ego-involved. This simply means you have a *belief* that your self-worth is dependent on being (or having others be) a certain way. Your expectations do not allow for mistakes. Relax. Life is full of making "mistakes."

Fortunately, little children have no concept of *mistake* when they fall down while learning to walk. They don't waste any time thinking about their fall. If they get hurt, they may cry for a few minutes before getting up and going on.

Someone once chided Thomas Edison by saying, "It is too bad you had so many failures before you were successful."

Edison replied, "I didn't have failures. I learned many things that did not work."

Understanding the principles helps you recapture that sense of wonder as you journey through life.

By simply giving you a direction or a point of reference on your treasure map, the four principles are like natural laws. The natural law of gravity includes no rule that you should not jump off a building; it simply explains what happens if you do. Similarly, the principle of thought as a function includes no rule that you should not think from your thought system; it simply explains what happens when you do.

Making mistakes in math is not disastrous. It does not even seem like a bother to go back over the figures to find the mistakes and correct them when you feel gratitude for the knowledge allowing you to do that. Knowing how to correct mistakes is simply part of the process; and, for some of us, not knowing how to use calculus does not mean we can't use addition or subtraction to make our lives easier. In the same way, a lack of deeper understanding of the principles does not keep you from experiencing the benefits of what you do know.

Although airplanes were (before computers) slightly off course more than they were exactly on course, pilots did not waste time fretting but simply used the principles of navigation to keep getting back on track.

When you see that everything is just as it should be, you will see that creating a programmed thought system is perfect—just as an *understanding* of the thought system is perfect. That troublesome thought system can be seen as a wonderful teacher when you acknowledge how many opportunities it gives you to learn wonderful life lessons.

Recently, I had thoughts that produced feelings of inadequacy. I found myself wondering, "Will these people like me? Why would they want to spend any time with me?" In the past, I either would have taken those thoughts seriously and withdrawn, pretending that I didn't care, or would have tried to show off in some way to make them like me. In this instance, I noticed the thoughts, dismissed them, and enjoyed myself with the inherent good feelings that arose from my heart. I learned how much I like myself when I dismiss my thought system—and thereby create an energy that is appealing to others. Next time, however, I may forget again, act on thoughts of inadequacy, and not enjoy myself.

The principles let me know when I am on course (because I feel great—or at least aware), and they let me know when I am off course. When I am able to dismiss the content of my thinking, I feel grateful. When I do not drop these thoughts, I continue to feel bad. When a bad mood seems to hang on, I have found it helpful to look for the life lesson and have found it helpful to use the process of "mirror insight."

MIRROR INSIGHT

What if you know everything you have read so far yet still can't let go of your negative feelings? Welcome to the club—and to a possibility for seeing your negative feelings as an opportunity to learn more about yourself. Your negative feelings may have a message for you that can provide you with a very important life lesson in order for healing to take place. Look in the mirror and see what there is about *you* that is being reflected by the circumstances you think are causing your negative feelings.

Recently, I was on a flight from Germany to Los Angeles. I did not want to check my luggage, a green roll-on case and a small duffle. I stored both pieces in the rack above my seat and settled down to read my novel.

I heard an announcement from a flight attendant that they had a green roll-on case that they would have to put off the plane if it was not claimed. I remember thinking, "That could be mine; I wonder if I should check it out." I dismissed the possibility, however, because I knew my case was stored in the rack. A few minutes before takeoff, I heard my name over the loudspeaker. The two people strapped into their seats next to me had to get up so I could struggle out to the aisle and seek a flight attendant. Another passenger hurried up to me and told me that the man behind me had taken my case out of the rack so that he would have room for his things. She was furious because he had left my case in the aisle, and everyone had had to climb over it. I couldn't believe it; but sure enough, when I went to the front of the plane, there was my green suitcase. I explained to the attendant what had happened, but there was not time or space enough to do anything except have my bag checked.

I was so angry at this man that I went back to my seat and confronted him: "What made you think you had the right to take my case out of the rack?" He spoke English very well and calmly explained, "It was above my seat, and you are supposed to put your luggage under your seat." (He hadn't bothered to notice that the rack over his seat also extended over my seat.) I couldn't believe it, nor could my fellow passenger, who had told me what had happened. She joined me in confronting him. We let him know that we thought he was inconsiderate, selfish, and arrogant. He shrugged it all off as though it were nothing.

I sat in my seat and fumed. I tried to tell myself, "Let it go. This is just your thoughts, and they are driving you crazy. Your anger isn't hurting him, but it is certainly hurting you." I remembered one of my favorite, anonymous quotations: "Anger does more damage to the vessel in which it is stored than to the object upon which it is poured." I also remembered all the scientific research about the damage that anger does to the body and to the immune system.

None of that helped. I continued to think about the audacity of this man. I could not understand how he could possibly justify his actions.

After dinner, I met several passengers in the aisle by the restrooms, and they all fed my self-righteousness. One man said, "What a jerk." I loved it. The woman who had already spoken to me said she was still so angry that she couldn't enjoy her meal. I loved it. I went back and told the man off some more.

Can you believe that someone who has written a book on *serenity* could act this way? What about dismissing the thought system and accessing inner wisdom? What about using my feelings as a compass to let me know that I was taking my thoughts very seriously?

Well, eventually I did pay attention to my feelings compass, and now I'm thankful to the man who gave me such a wonderful opportunity to learn more about myself and to heal the beliefs that were causing my misery.

> It is helpful to know that every upset provides an opportunity for learning life lessons and healing old programs.

I decided to do a meditation and try the mirror insight process to see what my anger was telling me about *myself*. My first glimpse in *the mirror* was to see that I had been a bit (just a bit) selfish and inconsiderate myself to bring two pieces of luggage onto the airplane. If everyone did the same, there wouldn't be enough storage room. It was easy to gloss over my own selfishness when his seemed so much worse.

Notice that last statement. This is the kind of thinking we use often to excuse ourselves from changing. "If someone else is worse, they are the ones who should change." The truth is that if our faults are not as bad, it should be easier for us to change. From the thought system, it makes more sense to point fingers instead of changing ourselves. From inner wisdom, we feel humility and drop our judgments.

This small insight, from looking into the mirror, took me into my heart where I felt gratitude to this man for giving me such an excellent opportunity to see myself. Whether or not he was right or wrong for moving my suitcase became a nonissue when I started to understand the message and life lesson my anger had for me. I felt compassion for both of us. I had to laugh at the drama I created from my thought system. I also felt grateful for the mirror insight process, which so often helps me find the gift in every situation.

When you use your feelings compass and discover that you are in your thought system, rather than judging or criticizing yourself, it is helpful to know that every upset provides an opportunity for learning life lessons and healing old programs.

Use your feelings compass to let you know where you are—in your thought system, or in your heart. If this simple awareness does not lead you to an immediate dismissal of your thought system, look in the mirror, find the gifts that can be found in your situation, or seek help to heal your programmed beliefs. One way or another, your feelings compass can point you in the right direction so that you can immediately or eventually find your way to your heart.

My present level of understanding has increased the amount of time I live from my heart. I would be foolish to believe the principles are invalid simply because I still sometimes get hooked by my programmed thought system; my understanding is not yet deep enough to save me every time. But my understanding *is* developed enough that I do not take those thoughts as seriously as I used to; I get quiet sooner, or I get help if I need it.

When you get *caught up* in your thought system, it is not helpful to feel guilt or blame or failure. It isn't helpful to fight your thoughts or to try to control them. This is like trying to control a whirlpool. If you fight and struggle when you get caught in a whirlpool, you will drown; if you relax and get very quiet, it will carry you down and spit you out at the bottom so that you can float to the surface. However, even with this knowledge, it could be difficult to relax in a whirlpool—even when the results of not relaxing could be death.

Unlike fighting a whirlpool, fighting thoughts that make you unhappy is not a life-and-death matter; it's just a matter of happiness or unhappiness. It might take faith to follow suggestions from others who understand the principles that lead to happiness, but once you experience results yourself, you will have access to the wisdom of your own experience.

I repeat: If you are still struggling with these ideas, it may be that you are trying to understand the principles from your thought system. Your reading this far indicates that your inner wisdom is also *hearing* despite your thoughts. *Understanding* may come from your heart when you least expect it. Not expecting it may mean that you have quit thinking about it (quit struggling) so that your inner wisdom and inspiration can surface.

Confusion can be a good sign of progress; it may mean your thought system is being scrambled. This is a good time to drop thought and stop trying to figure it out. Leave room for messages from your heart.

HOW LONG DOES IT TAKE TO UNDERSTAND?

Sometimes a deep *understanding* of these principles comes in an instant; sometimes it takes longer. Some people have the impression that *understanding* is an all-or-nothing event, which it can be. It can also be a gradual process of levels of understanding. *Understanding* is actually moment to moment. You may have under-standing at one moment and cover it up with thoughts the next. Or you may have under-standing in certain areas and lack understanding in others. In either case, your feelings compass will let you know. When you experience your natural good feelings, you are coming from understanding; when you experience negative

> Gaining deeper understanding can be seen as an exciting life process leading us to increased experiences of joy and serenity until we are ready for permanent understanding.

emotions, you are coming from your illusions of the past and a lack of understanding of the truth in the present.

For many of us, understanding deepens as we keep listening from our hearts. As our understanding deepens, we find more joy and serenity in life.

For me, understanding was not instantaneous. When I first heard these principles, in my heart I knew they were true, but my thought system drove me crazy for a year and a half with objections and questions—"yes, but" and "how about" and "what if." Even though my old thought system kept getting in the way of my under-standing, my heart and inner wisdom kept leading me back to hear more, and gradually my "yes, buts" changed to "Of course. It is so simple, so obvious, so wonderful." Before *understanding*, everything can seem heavy and complicated; with *understanding*, everything is lighter and simpler.

The learning never ends. Once we get pointed in this direction, life just keeps getting nicer and nicer. Life keeps improving even when there is complete satisfaction with the way things are. George Pransky uses a graphic analogy to explain this phenomenon: It is like waiting at a bus stop for the bus to deeper understanding but having such a nice time at the bus stop that you don't care if the bus doesn't come. This kind of serenity and satisfaction is found only when we experience life from our hearts.

Most people do not experience permanent understanding. We might miss valuable opportunities for continuous learning if we did. It is nice to have at least enough understanding to know, at some level, that there are gifts to be found from the experiences we have when stuck in our thought system. It is nice to have enough understanding that it is difficult to take our thoughts as totally seriously as we would without some level of understanding. It is nice to have enough understanding that we don't judge ourselves or others when we become prisoners of our self-created thought system. Gaining deeper understanding can be seen as an exciting life process leading us to increased experiences of joy and serenity until we are ready for permanent understanding.

SUGGESTIONS

It doesn't matter if you choose not to follow any of the suggestions proposed in this book; their only purpose is to help you see the principles. If you don't see the wisdom behind the suggestions, they will appear to be just

more "rules" and "shoulds" and will only create more insecurity, burdens, arguments, or other dissatisfaction. If a
suggestion doesn't inspire insight from your inner wisdom, it's all right. Don't *think* about it; just keep *listening*
from your heart, and inspired insight will creep up on
you when you least expect it.

Suggestions about what to "do" will be meaningful
only if you feel confirmation in your heart. When you
feel the truth in your heart, the suggestions may trigger
your own insight. You may feel something like, "Of
course! That makes sense, and I know exactly how this
applies to my life."

Heart confirmation means that you have captured
the feeling rather than the words. That feeling may lead
you to follow the suggestions in this book (or possibly to
do something much different) from your own inner wisdom. You will then be well on your way because no one
knows how to solve your problems better than you do
when you dismiss your thought system and have access to
your heart and inner wisdom. The whole point of this
book is to help you know that.

Follow the wisdom of your heart, and what to do
will be obvious. Your inherent good feelings will guide
you to eliminate stress and to find serenity in your life
and in your relationships.

CHAPTER NINE

What Thoughts Are You Willing to Give Up Your Happiness For?

One day I put a nice oak table in the garage for storage. Other family members started putting their junk on the table. I nagged, "Don't put your things on the oak table, or it will get scratched." No one listened, and eventually everything from tools and bicycle parts to a worn-out car battery were on the table.

Finally, I went into the garage and cleaned off all the junk so that I could cover the table with something to protect it. Sure enough, it was scratched and gouged.

I was angry! Fortunately, I had some errands to do, so no one had to listen to me. I drove around, totally lost in my negative thoughts—taking them very seriously.

Finally, my feelings compass let me know that my anger was making me feel upset and miserable. As soon as

I became aware of what I was doing to myself with my thoughts, my mood changed. I had to laugh as I began to see things differently.

From my heart, I usually have a wonderful sense of humor. I realized my family had not been irresponsible for putting things on the table; I had been irresponsible for not protecting it in the first place.

Then my insight let me see that I was living my life for scratches in an oak table when there were so many other, much nicer possibilities. It was a beautiful day, and I had been missing it. I had so many things to be grateful for, and I was taking them all for granted. A question came from my inner wisdom: "What thoughts are you willing to give up your happiness for?"

Everyone who hears this story thinks it is funny that I didn't "see the obvious" and have enough sense to cover the table in the first place. This is the point. Silly thinking is usually obvious to anyone who is not caught up in it. When we are caught up in a certain way of interpreting the world, it seems like the only possible reality.

When we are angry, all we see is a world full of bitterness. When we are loving, we see a world full of love, beauty, compassion, forgiveness, gratitude, and peace of mind. *What we think is what we get!*

Have you ever had the experience of feeling very sorry for yourself about something and then hearing about someone who has or is experiencing a "real" tragedy? Suddenly, you realized that your circumstances were nothing in comparison and not worth worrying about. (I don't mean to imply that there are "real" circumstances that make worry more valid than wisdom from the heart. The point is that even insignificant things can cause misery when seen through the thought system.)

Think of something that is bothering you. Then go to chapter 5 and look at the Feelings Compass Chart on page 44. It is likely that you will see the source of your misery somewhere in the column on the right. Thoughts based on any of the concepts in the right column will cause unhappiness. Are any of them worth giving up your happiness for? As soon as you realize that you do not want to hang on to thoughts based in that column, any or all of the four principles can lead you back to serenity, love, and happiness.

WHICH PRINCIPLE IS THE MOST IMPORTANT?

All the principles are interrelated, and any one can come first. Sometimes you will see beauty everywhere because you are in a good mood (a high level of consciousness). Other times, when you are caught up in negative thinking, remembering that thoughts are just thoughts will raise your level of consciousness, and you will see things differently.

Sometimes, when you think you are *right* about something, remembering the fact of separate realities may create humility, and you will then see different realities as interesting rather than as right or wrong. Another time, you may use your feelings as a compass to let you know you are off track. That *understanding* alone may take you out of your thought system and into your heart—or at least let you know you need to get quiet until the thoughts pass and leave room for inspiration and wisdom.

QUIET

Quiet is not necessarily an absence of action but an absence of negative thoughts running wild in a thought system that takes them seriously. True quiet is not always something that one "does." It may be a feeling of serenity as you go about your daily tasks, or it may be a simple awareness of your thoughts and where they are coming from. Quiet can be enhanced by something you do, such as meditating, walking in nature, or consciously feeling gratitude for the many miracles in your life.

> Quiet is the humility you feel in the absence of negative thoughts and beliefs. In this quiet and humble state of mind, you will have a different experience of life.

With *understanding*, quiet is natural. Before understanding, it makes sense to actively quiet yourself because slowing down can make it easier to listen to your feelings compass. Getting physically quiet may help you hear the messages from your heart.

Quiet is one of the naturally good feelings you have when you dismiss negative thoughts. If negative thoughts are inspiring frenetic activity *to prove something*, then that activity will also be dismissed, and you will *feel* and *be* serene.

Being quiet does not mean sacrificing productivity; instead, you will simply be more selective, from your heart, in what you want to produce. You will also be much more efficient when negative thoughts are not interfering and blinding you to your inner wisdom.

Quiet is the humility you feel in the absence of negative thoughts and beliefs. In this quiet and humble state of mind, you will have a different experience of life. The world looks very different when seen through feelings of love, gratitude, and compassion—for yourself and others.

True quiet is total humility—not an attribute of a programmed thought system. Because quiet is such an important path to *understanding* the principles, it is covered more extensively in the next chapter. As you read these words, you may be *feeling* the truth of them. Then you may wonder, "Since this is so obvious and simple, why does it seem so difficult at times? Using the computer as an analogy may shed some light on the conditioning that has such a strong influence on programming thought systems.

THE BRAIN AS A COMPUTER

The brain is like a perfect computer, but it, too, is only as useful as the software put into it and the person's ability to operate it. Using your programmed thought system is the same as using old, outdated software—full of "bugs." It is also the same as trying to operate a computer without understanding the basic principles or reading the instructions. Both produce unsatisfactory results. You are now reading the instructions and gaining an understanding of the principles that can help you eliminate or bypass old, outdated software (your programmed thought system) so you can produce beautiful results in your life.

Many people do not realize that their thoughts and beliefs are not *themselves*, just as software is not the computer. I have seen several versions of a cartoon showing someone smashing a computer because it wouldn't "work" properly. When we take our negative thoughts and beliefs seriously, we are using as much sense as the cartoon character. We have forgotten that it is our thought system that is full of bugs. Our thinking *ability* is flawless.

> Many people do not realize that their thoughts and beliefs are not *themselves*, just as software is not the computer.

Computer buffs know what happens when they try to feed new information into a software program not designed to understand it: the computer beeps and flashes the words "syntax error" or even worse, "fatal error" on the screen. Even though the new information could improve tremendously the capabilities of the software program, it simply cannot accept the data.

Your brain often does the same thing with new information that could be very useful to you. When you try to filter this information through your thought system, it "beeps" and says, "wrong!" Fortunately, you have something a computer does not have—a heart full of inner wisdom to let you know what new information is useful to improve your life and relationships and what information is not useful. You don't have access to your heart and inner wisdom, however, until you dismiss the thought system. Dismissing thoughts does not leave a void; it clears the channel so thinking can be used to express heart messages and natural good feelings.

There is a major difference between humans and computers: Computers cannot function without software, whereas humans function best without their thought systems. Another major difference is how software is programmed.

SOFTWARE (PROGRAMMED THOUGHT SYSTEM)

Computer software is written by people with knowledge of computer language. The computer industry is mushrooming as knowledge increases and applications multiply. Old software is thrown out as improved software is designed. Wouldn't it be wonderful if we could throw out our old software when it becomes outdated? Actually, that is just what happens when we dismiss our thought systems and live from our hearts. However, there is a reason we sometimes don't do this or that it doesn't always last when we do.

Unfortunately, the largest portion of our programmed thought system is created when we are very young and lacking in knowledge. Much of our program comes from the decisions we make (thoughts and beliefs we create) in response to the parenting methods we experienced. (This is not meant to blame parents but to understand the process of how a thought system is created.) Sibling interactions may have an even bigger influence on our decisions than our parents as we try to figure out what we need to do to "find our place" in the family.[1]

In our parenting workshops, we point out that children are always making decisions (at a subconscious level) about who they are, what the world is like, and what they need to do (how they need to behave) in this world to thrive or to survive. Since many of these decisions are made on the basis of a child's fear of disapproval and/or punishment (and how to find belonging and significance in the family), many decisions have to do with surviving instead of thriving. These decisions may have made sense when we were children. The problem is that we hang on to these decisions when they no longer serve us.

Valerie Seeman Moreton describes this process in her book *Heal the Cause:*

> Anytime we make a decision with great emotion attached, it becomes the subconscious "rule of action" from that time forth. This means that when an upset occurs, even at a very young age, like one or two, a decision is made (subconsciously) that influences the rest of your life. If that decision was that you were "not loved" or "not good enough," your whole life would be about compensating for that belief to prove it was false. Behaving in a particular way to get love or approval can cause self-defeating patterns to develop and defense mechanisms to form. And all of this is based upon a lie, founded upon fear instead of love.[2]

---

1. For more information on the effects of birth order on our thought system, see chapter 3 of *Positive Discipline* (New York: Ballantine, 1997).
2. Valerie Seeman Moreton, N.D., *Heal the Cause* (San Diego: Kalos Publishing, 1996).

Many defense mechanisms take the form of misbe-havior. Through experiential activities (where parents role-play their children), adults gain an understanding about how the thought system is formed—theirs and their children's. They also learn that the best way to help a "misbehaving child" change beliefs and behavior is through love (encouragement), not fear (punishment). Love can take both parent and child out of their thought systems and into their hearts, where effective solutions can be found.

As adults, we also "misbehave" when fear creates de-fense mechanisms. You don't experience fear when you access your heart or spiritual source. Fear comes only from the illusions of old programming in the thought system. When you have difficulty "throwing away" old, outdated programming, it could be that subconscious decisions and beliefs have not been brought into your awareness and healed. It could be that you have not yet learned the life lesson or seen the gifts that can be found in your situation. Learning the lesson (seeing the gift) can immediately take you out of your thought system and into your heart.

SEEING THE LESSONS

There are many master teachers and scientists who teach that there is divine order to everything. Perhaps shifting back and forth between your thought system and heart increases your appreciation for happiness and peace of mind. Perhaps you could not learn important life lessons any other way.

Not long ago, I was using my thought system in a way that was making me miserable. Because I thought a friend was being inconsiderate, I was upset; my stomach was churning, and I couldn't sleep. When my feelings compass let me know what I was doing, I clearly saw that I was giving up my happiness for some negative thoughts. My awareness was followed by a message from my heart inviting me to look in the mirror and see the lessons I could learn from my experience: *Which is worse, being inconsiderate, or being judgmental?* I had to laugh at my self-righteousness. Then I saw that it was not even a matter of being better or worse because being inconsiderate and judgmental are both simply aspects of thought-provoked insecurity from a programmed thought system.

Perspective and compassion quickly followed as I remembered the many times I have been inconsiderate either because I didn't know better or because I *believed* I was justified. I also realized that just because I *thought* this friend was being inconsiderate didn't mean she was; it meant only that she was not living up to some rules and beliefs *I had created* from my programmed thought system. I laughed at those thoughts also and could then feel love and gratitude for my friend—and for myself. I had learned, again, that there are not any thoughts I am willing to give up my happiness for.

When happiness is more important to you than anything else, you will be happy because there will be no thoughts for which you will be willing to give up your happiness. You will do whatever it takes to get out of your thought system and into your heart.

CHAPTER TEN

Quiet

An *understanding* of the principles can lead to quiet, or quiet can lead to an *understanding* of the principles. It has been mentioned often that getting quiet is an excellent way to dismiss the thought system, or at least to wait patiently until it loses its hold over you.

Getting quiet can mean many things. It can mean simply staring out the window, taking a nap, reading a book, or anything that distracts you from the busyness of your programmed thought system. Another way to get quiet is through meditation.

Meditation can lead to the ultimate quiet for some people (going into "the silence," or "the gap between thoughts"). For others, meditation may be a time to sit quietly as a simple exercise in an awareness of the busy thought system, for deep relaxation, or to listen to messages or inspiration from their heart or spiritual source.

MEDITATION

For years I wanted to meditate but *thought* I couldn't do it. Every time I tried to meditate in groups, I would either go to sleep, or my legs would twitch, or I just couldn't make my mind get quiet. When I tried to meditate by myself, it drove me crazy to sit for five minutes, let alone twenty. I just couldn't do it. Listen to that language. I "couldn't"? Well, it sure seemed that way.

> Meditation is a wonderful way to get quiet if you leave your expectations and judgments behind. It can be a vehicle that takes you to your heart or spiritual source.

I now meditate for at least twenty minutes almost every day. How did I get from there to here? It took commitment based on my understanding of the importance of a quiet mind to access my heart and my spiritual source. Because of this commitment, I took three weeks out of my life to go to a wonderful retreat. While there, I made the commitment to sit for twenty minutes—no matter what. I was prepared to listen to the chatter of my mind for twenty minutes if that's all that happened.

The first day I was peeking at my watch every five minutes. The second day I went fifteen minutes before I peeked. But instead of feeling energized, as I had been led to expect, I found that I was totally wiped out. So, I took a nap. The third day, I scheduled a walk into nature after my meditation so that I could wake up. By the fourth or fifth day, I stopped peeking at my watch, and meditation began to feel wonderful.

I gave up all my expectations (except for my commitment to sit for twenty minutes), and then all the expectations I had given up started to happen. That may sound like double-talk, but I now know that not being attached to expectations allows them room to happen—or not. And that is what my meditations are like. Sometimes I receive profound messages from my heart or spiritual source. Other times I simply feel love and comfort. Simply! The chatter of my mind comes and goes. I just let it be. (Well, sometimes when the chatter gets too aggravating, I may take deep breaths or concentrate on love and gratitude.)

Meditation is a wonderful way to get quiet if you leave your expectations and judgments behind. It can be a vehicle that takes you to your heart or spiritual source. During this time of quiet, you may simply be aware of your thoughts. You may experience your inherent good feelings of love, gratitude, and joy. You may receive inspiration or specific messages regarding a life concern.

During one of my meditations, I received the following message: *What is insight except sight from within? Walking through life without insight from your heart and your spiritual source is like walking through life with your eyes closed.*

On my next nature walk, I tried walking with my eyes closed. Try it sometime. Find a path where there are no other people, if you can, and try walking with your eyes closed. What happens? Do you feel fear, mistrust, disorientation, insecure? How long can you keep going before you have to open your eyes? Remember, this is on a path where there are no other distractions. What happens when you try walking with your eyes closed on a busy sidewalk or on a busy street? I realized that I am usually going through life thinking my eyes are wide open, when in truth my thoughts have created many illusions that distract me from my inner peace and produce fear, mistrust, disorientation, and insecurity. I am literally *in the dark*. *Understanding* the principles is like turning on the light. Quiet through mediation can facilitate *understanding*.

Anyone who says they don't have time to meditate is saying they don't have time to open the eyes of their hearts—that they would prefer to go through life in the dark.

How much of the movie do you see when the video is on fast-forward? Living your life without meditation is like keeping the VCR on fast-forward. You are missing the movie of your life. Put the video on pause, take time for meditation, and see how much more present you will be in the story of your own life.

CHORE MEDITATION

You can experience a state of meditation without sitting quietly. You can bring a state of meditation into your daily living.

Think of a chore you'd rather not do—for example, washing the dishes. Take a deep breath and quiet your mind. Then wash the dishes with love. Avoid rushing. Be fully in the moment and bring joy to every movement. Then bring your gratitude to the task. It is amazing how much you can find to be grateful for: the nourishing food you ate, the wonderful invention of running water, your nice dishes. Be grateful for this opportunity to bring a state of meditation into everything you do.

NATURE

Quiet can be enhanced in nature. We need nature in our lives to ground us, to nurture us, to give us messages (yes, nature will talk with you—more about that later), and to bring us to joy and gratitude.

We all love to be in nature, whether we are in a park, near the ocean, in the mountains, or near a stream, lake, or pond. We all feel rejuvenated and renewed in those special places. We feel relaxed and peaceful. Yet most of our time in life is spent in our busyness away from nature. In fact, some people take their busy minds with them when they go into nature and rob themselves of nature's soothing energy.

For those who live in an urban environment, taking the time to be in nature is essential. Likewise, those who live in more rural areas need to take the time to appreciate the beauty and simplicity of nature that surrounds them instead of taking it for granted.

Do you remember those times as a child when you would spend hours fascinated with one miracle of nature after another? Remember the times you would watch a bird in flight and wonder what it would feel like to fly, or lie for hours on a grassy hillside and watch clouds take all kinds of shapes? Can you remember how fascinating it was to watch a spider spin its web or to watch how the ants were so intent with purpose and order in their work? You may have marveled at the beauty of a plant or flower and just immersed yourself in the scent of it. And the ocean: Can you remember marveling at the vastness of that body of water and the immense power it has—and your joy as you played with the waves or your content-ment as you built a sand castle? (Many children today are missing these experiences because of their overly sched-uled lives.)

Try taking your childlike wonder back into nature. Take time to watch it, and feel it, and enjoy it. Many of us have simply forgotten about the importance of nature and how it truly feeds us to our core. Is that busyness of every-day living so important that we don't even have enough time to feed ourselves prop-erly? We need to examine our priorities. Sometimes old platitudes are worth remem-bering—are we taking time to smell the roses?

One way to become more aware of how to con-nect with the earth and na-ture is to learn what the history of Native Americans has to teach us. The Native Americans were completely connected with nature. They lived off the land just as the animals do. They knew the uses of all the plants and animals and had respect and a feeling of gratitude for what the earth, their mother, was providing for them. Showing respect and reverence for the earth, nature, and the animals that provided them with food was part of their sacred rituals.

Many of us, and our children, have completely lost touch with the joys of nature. Many years ago, my family and I rented a camper and went to Sequoia National Park

> Nature is calling to all of us who are willing to listen. Our lives are enriched tremen-dously when we leave technology and our busy minds behind and take time to spend with nature.

for a week. For the first two days, the children were miserable. They were devastated that they couldn't watch television. They complained that there was nothing to do. We tried to convince them that there was plenty to do out in the woods, but that possibility seemed beyond their comprehension.

Eventually, however, they became bored with boredom and began to poke their heads outside. It wasn't long before they heard the call of nature. They played in the streams, climbed trees, created huts in the woods, gathered wood for the fire pit, went on hikes, played games with sticks and rocks, and chased squirrels. They were so alive. At the end of the week, they didn't want to leave.

There is an important lesson for all of us in the experience of these children. Nature is calling to all of us who are willing to listen. Our lives are enriched tremendously when we leave technology and our busy minds behind and take time to spend with nature.

Everyone can find a place to go and commune with nature. It could be a city park, the beach, the woods, the desert, or anywhere in the countryside. Find a rock to sit on, a tree to lean on, or grass to lie on and let yourself be open to the nurturing energy of nature. Be open to messages you can receive from the wind and the sun. Sometimes you may want to ask a tree, a rock, a leaf, or any part of nature what message it has for you. Take a notepad and pencil so that you can record the message.

At workshops I have shared this possibility with many people.[1] When I explain the exercise, some think I

---

1. I was first introduced to this exercise in a workshop with Jack and Deborah Bartello. For information on their workshops call, 1-800-446-5959.

must be kidding. But when they come back after doing the exercise, they are humbled. The insights they have gained into themselves and the messages they have received are truly inspiring. As they read their messages to each other, we sometimes have to pass the Kleenex box, for people are truly moved and often see how the message someone else received is also helpful to themselves. You might experience personal benefit from the following messages one person found from nature:

Message from a Stump

I am a tree stump—being what I am.

I don't care about judgments of others.

Some may say I don't have the magnificence of the tall, strong tree I once was,

But it doesn't matter.

Part of me was chopped down and hauled away—for some good use, I am sure.

I am still beautiful.

Look at my patterns—in my bark, in my bare wood.

—in the niches and crevices where bugs find refuge.

You may stand on me, or sit on me and bask in the sun.

My message to you about love: There is nothing to be except who you are.

Look closely and see the beauty of who you are.

You might enjoy keeping a "nature's messages" journal. Write down the messages you receive from different parts of nature. One day it may be a tree. Another day it may be a leaf, a raindrop, a twig, a pond, a mountain, sand, or a rock. The possibilities are endless—as are the messages.

SPIRITUAL MESSAGES EVERYWHERE

Spiritual messages can also be found in everything that happens to you. For example, on my walk one morning I was listening to some music on my small tape player. The earphones started to buzz. I wondered what the spiritual message could be. It was so obvious: *Your mind is buzzing away all the time. Don't let it interfere. Just let it be and enjoy the music. You don't have to make your thoughts go away. Just don't give them so much energy, and other information will get through.* An amazing thing happened. The buzzing in the microphone stopped. Another amazing thing happened. My buzzing thoughts didn't stop. I'm joking, of course—it's not at all amazing that my thoughts kept buzzing. They never stop. But how nice to know that I don't have to pay so much attention to them.

When we are open to spiritual messages, they can be found anytime we are willing to receive them.

Let's tackle a seemingly difficult situation. Suppose someone with whom you think you are very much in love leaves you. What kind of spiritual message could there possibly be in that? Could it be that there is something better in store for you—perhaps a better relationship or an occasion to learn how much you can enjoy being by yourself? Or could it be that your spiritual source knows that it is not good for you to be with this person?

We have all heard stories about people who believed that being abandoned by their spouse was the worst thing that could ever happen to them, until time passed (sometimes years) and they came to see that the spouse leaving was the *best* thing that could have happened to them.

We can't hear spiritual messages when we give more credibility to our egos and programmed beliefs than we do to our spiritual sources. And that is okay. We are ready when we are ready.

If you aren't ready to see spiritual messages in so-called catastrophic events, start with less emotional events. Suppose you are taking a walk and you come to a big hill. You are tired and *think* you can't make it. Tune in to the message from the hill. The first question you might ask is, "Do I really *want* to climb this hill?" Maybe it is time to turn around and go in another direction. If you do want to climb the hill, you may get other messages, such as "Slow down. What's the hurry? Take time to rest. Go one step at a time. Pause and look at the beautiful scenery all around you." Another message could be that the difficult climb will strengthen your muscles and help you become more fit. Then comes the fun part. Notice how all those messages may fit perfectly in your life. Focus on a life problem you are having. See if any of the messages would be helpful.

> Awareness leads to understanding, or understanding leads to awareness. You can then be open to seeing the gift in all things.

APPRECIATION WALKS

Try an appreciation walk. Tune in with appreciation and gratitude for everything you see. Sometimes your focus may be close to the ground. Other times you may focus on horizons and vistas. You may be drawn to focus on birds or other animals. Notice the breezes or wind, the sun, or any sounds of nature. You may focus on short distances, long distances, or anywhere in between. Notice how much there is to see and appreciate. See how long you can go before you lose your focus on nature and become distracted by the busyness of your mind. Do not judge yourself or anything that happens—just become aware.

SELF-DEFEATING BELIEFS AND BEHAVIORS

In her book *A Return to Love*, Marianne Williamson confirms what happens when we forget that we created our own thought system and ego:

> Not everyone chooses to heed the call of his own heart. As all of us are only too aware, the loud and frantic voices of the outer world easily drown out the small still loving voice within.[2]

Many of us who seek quiet use the ego of our thought system to defeat ourselves in many ways. Four ways to consider are expectations, self-defeating judgments, lack of awareness, and not seeing the gift in all things.

Expectations

George had a great meditation. He felt connected to his soul. He felt love and joy. The energy was so strong that

---

2. Marianne Williamson, *A Return to Love* (New York: Harper Paperbacks, 1992), p. 35.

he walked around in bliss for a day. The next morning, he meditated and was very disappointed. His experience was nothing like the day before. He spent the rest of that day in total depression. What had happened?

George's expectations got in the way. He wanted his second meditation to be just like the first. George wasn't aware of it, but his expectations had become part of his programmed thought system.

Self-Defeating Judgments

Then George allowed his judgments to take over. He beat up on himself for not having a "high enough" level of consciousness to meditate "right." He compared himself to others who surely had better meditation experiences than he did—all the time.

Lack of Awareness

Of course, George wasn't aware that it was his *expectations* and *judgments* that were creating blocks. If he had been aware of this, his judgments would have been defused and he could have been open to his heart. Judgments can't take over unless we let them. We let them take over when we forget that they don't have a life of their own—we create them. Awareness leads to understanding, or understanding leads to awareness. You can then be open to seeing the gift in all things.

Not Seeing the Gift in All Things

George had heard about seeing the gift in all things. The third day he sat in meditation and asked his heart to show him the gift in what he was experiencing. He soon received an insight about his expectations and his judgments—and he chuckled. He then realized how often he let his expectations and judgments keep him from seeing the gifts in his life experiences. He still did not have the same experience as his meditation on the first day, but he didn't compare them. He felt total joy in what he did experience.

Another message that came to him was, *What is, IS.* He had heard that before, but now it had new meaning for him. He knew that on some days he may not receive any messages at all but that sitting quietly during his meditation time would be enough—a beautiful gift. When he felt blocked, he would tune into the blocks and see if they had anything to teach him.

Is it starting to sound as though the same battles are fought over and over—the battle between the ego and the heart? Does it sometimes seem as though the thought system and messages from the world were created solely to take you away from your heart and spiritual experiences? They were and they weren't, depending on your perspective. From your heart you can see that the world and your thought system give you many opportunities to strengthen your spiritual experience. The sooner you can see the gift in all things, the sooner you experience love and gratitude.

GLIMPSES ARE ENOUGH

It seems to be the human condition to spend more time experiencing life through our programmed thought systems than from our hearts. While we are learning, it is helpful to appreciate the glimpses. Every glimpse into *understanding* is like money in the bank that we can draw on when we need it.

While writing this book, I had a huge glimpse into the serenity and peace of mind that comes from *understanding*. I felt so loving and such joy and gratitude that it seemed that nothing could disturb my peace.

I was given a big test. I had paid a typesetter over $1,000, in advance, to complete a revision of one of my self-published books. One day I dropped by to see how she was doing. I learned that the company had gone into some kind of bankruptcy and that someone from the court system came by every day to collect their daily receipts. Part of the bankruptcy agreement was that they had to collect a certain amount of money to hand over to the court, or they would lose their business completely. So, they would work on projects for which they could collect money when they were finished—instead of projects for which the money had been received in advance and was long gone. My friends and family could hardly believe how undisturbed I was by this news. I honestly believed that it would all turn out for the best—even if I lost the money. From this state of mind, I discussed the situation very calmly and lovingly with the woman who was working on the typesetting. I did not blame her or get angry with her. I empathized with her and the conditions under which she had to work.

She stayed late and worked on her own time to finish my project. She later told me that my energy was so encouraging to her that she wanted to do all she could to help me.

I wish I could say that I was able to stay in that state of mind. I have since let other situations disturb my peace. However, that experience is "in the bank." I love to remember it and draw on its energy as a reminder that, no matter what happens, I have a choice to deal with any situation from love or from fear.

Glimpses are truly wonderful gifts. Be gentle with yourself while you are strengthening your *understanding*, and be gentle while you are learning to get quiet and hear the messages from your heart.

CHAPTER ELEVEN

Contrary to Popular Opinion

Since your programmed thought system is full of many beliefs that block your inner wisdom, you will see things differently from the mainstream of popular opinion when you have access to your heart. One of the beliefs perpetuated by popular opinion is that you need rules to live by.

RULES

As your *understanding* deepens, you will realize that when living from your heart or spiritual source, you need no rules. Rules are based on thoughts that create fear. Some people fear that without rules, anarchy would prevail— rape, murder, lying, cheating, and stealing. This is not true. Most people would not consider inhumane acts even if there were no laws against them. And people who do are not stopped by laws. Thought-produced insecurity creates negative behavior. People enjoying their inner wisdom do positive things naturally—without rules.

When your heart is blocked, you don't listen when your inner wisdom tries to get through and tell you, "This rule does not make sense." If you listened, you would see that the rule is often based on judgments of right and wrong instead of love and encouragement. Most people usually ignore this inner guidance, hearing instead their thoughts saying, "You are not following this rule well enough." They then feel inadequate, frustrated, depressed, and more insecure, creating a vicious cycle. Other people "rebel" against the rules instead of following their hearts to do what makes sense in a positive manner.

It makes no sense to rely on rules when you have access to your inner wisdom and inspiration. As your heart guides you through each day, you will experience positive results and enjoy life. It will not lead you astray.

Although much of what I have been teaching may sound like rules, there is a great difference between principles and rules. A principle is like a road map: it does not include rules about where you *should* go but lets you know where you are or where you will end up, depending on which direction you travel. If you are in Virginia and want to go to New York, it makes no sense to go south. Likewise, if you are feeling bad and want to feel good, it makes no sense to use your thought system and take your negative thoughts seriously.

By turning any of the examples or suggestions into rules, you make them a part of your thought system, changing them beyond the recognition of your inner wisdom. They are no longer principles.

Rules are like "shoulds," with a sense of punishment and reward attached. Principles are natural laws, which simply let us understand the natural consequences of what we do.

When we listen from our hearts, we *hear* principles rather than rules.

DOING

What you do is a direct result of your state of mind. When you allow your natural good feelings to surface (by dismissing negative thoughts), your state of mind is one of love, gratitude, and compassion. In this happy state of mind, you have access to inspiration, common sense, and wisdom. What you do from a happy state of mind will therefore be different from what you do in the state of mind that you create through the filters of your thought system.

When you are *nice* because you think that is how you "should" behave, there will be a nagging dissatisfaction. Often there are strings attached—expectations such as "If I am nice, then things should turn out my way" or "then people will love me." The world looks and feels different when you get beyond your thought system. When you are *nice* because it feels like the natural thing to do, you will experience satisfaction and contentment. There are no strings attached. There is true joy in the doing. Receiving love doesn't seem to be an issue; you find so much pleasure in loving.

Sometimes you may feel inspired to do something nice, but your thoughts sneak in and turn it into a "should." You will know this has happened when your feelings change from peaceful to stressed and anxious or resentful. A friend shared how this had happened to her. She loves baking cookies for friends and family during the holidays, but one year she realized it was no longer fun because she felt that she *should* bake cookies for what had become a long list of people. What she had started from her heart crossed over to her thought system, and the joy was gone.

We live in a very speeded up world. There is so much *doing* going on and not enough *being*. The thought system thrives in a busy world.

> The greatest thing you can do for yourself and your relationships is to take care of yourself and to *be happy.*

Your inner wisdom is always with you, but you can't listen to it if you don't slow down. I want to stress again that slowing down does not mean you have to be bored or non-productive, as illustrated in the following fairy tale.

A FAIRY TALE OF TWO PRINCESSES

Once upon a time there were two princesses, Princess Dew and Princess Bee.

Princess Dew was very busy running around doing things for other people, trying to make them happy. Some people loved what Princess Dew did for them, but instead of being happy, they just wanted more. Princess

Dew tried hard to do more for them, hoping that some-day they would be happy. Other people did not like what she did for them "for their own good" and wished she would stop interfering.

Princess Dew became worn-out, bitter, and frus-trated because people did not appreciate all she did for them. She was very unhappy. No one wanted to be around her.

Princess Bee was also very busy—being happy. She enjoyed everything: rainbows and clouds, rainy days and sunny days. She especially enjoyed people. She loved watching them "be." People loved being around her. Her happiness was contagious.

SERVICE

The fairy tale of Princess Bee and Princess Dew is not meant to suggest that we should not do things for others. A happy state of mind will probably inspire you to be of service to others in any way you can. What you do, however, will not come from "shoulds" or ulterior motives, and it will not be conditional. Service will be for the joy of the moment.

You will also know when to be of service to yourself. Taking care of yourself is not selfish when it is inspired from your inner wisdom. The greatest thing you can do for yourself and your relationships is to take care of yourself and to *be happy*.

SELFISHNESS

It is popular to have strong negative opinions about selfishness, and, in fact, the self-centeredness that comes from the thought system looks and feels like the popular descriptions. The self-interest that comes from inner wisdom and a happy state of mind, however, has a different look and feel.

I know this sounds like double-talk—until you see the difference, which is in the feeling. Selfishness from the thought system is based on ego, self-importance, resentment, rebellion, or total disregard for others; self-interest from a natural, happy state of mind is based on feelings of love and the joy of living. With these feelings, you will want to do whatever your inner wisdom leads you to do to enjoy life.

Because of your old beliefs about selfishness, you could let your thought system convince you that doing what you want is "selfish." If you stick to following the feeling from your inner wisdom, however, you will know the difference—no matter what anyone else thinks.

One day Mary felt like going for a nice, long walk. She received a message from her thought system: "You should not go for a walk when you have so many other things to do, like cleaning the house and shopping." She dismissed her thoughts and listened to her heart. She went for a walk and enjoyed the beautiful day. Her family came home to a happy wife and mother. They enjoyed being around her and felt her love.

Martha also wanted to go for a walk, but she listened to the "shoulds" from her thought system. She felt depressed and did not get much cleaning done. Her family came home to an unhappy wife and mother.

> You will know when decisions are inspiration from your inner wisdom when you start trusting your heart.

If you are asking, "How will anything ever get done if we always do what we want instead of doing what really needs to be done?" you have missed the point. The next day Martha went for a walk but still felt depressed. Mary stayed home and cleaned house and still felt happy.

From a happy feeling, Mary is able to know what is important for her own well-being and that of her family. From an unhappy feeling, Martha will feel dissatisfied no matter what she does. For example, Martha has trouble getting her children to do their chores, while Mary has inspiration for how to win the cooperation of her children. When Mary cleans house, it is because she enjoys a clean house, not because she is compulsive or following "shoulds." When Martha cleans the house, she is trying to prove that she is a good wife and mother.

When you enjoy a nice life, you will be creating serenity in your home and in the world.

Happiness and peace of mind are contagious.

DECISIONS

Contrary to popular opinion, it is not helpful to figure things out or make decisions when feeling stress. This only keeps you deeply enmeshed in your thought system. It is as ineffective as keeping your foot on the gas pedal to get out of a ditch while the spinning wheel digs deeper and deeper into the sand.

If you have any doubts about what to do, or if you want to do something because of negative feelings such as anger, let that be your clue that you are lost in your thought system. Get quiet and wait for your negative feelings to pass so your inner wisdom can surface.

Decisions from your heart are always positive and produce good results. You will know when decisions are inspiration from your inner wisdom when you start trusting your heart. You will not doubt their appropriateness—despite the messages from your thought system. You may not make decisions quickly, but you will make them with certainty.

Actually, the concept of decision making changes with an understanding of the principles. The familiar concept of decision making implies choice or effort. With understanding, decisions feel more like obvious, commonsense things to do than like choices or efforts.

Deepak Chopra discusses this as "The Law of Least Effort," the fourth of *The Seven Spiritual Laws of Success*:

> Least effort is expended when your actions are motivated by love, because nature is held together by the energy of love. When you seek power and control over other people, you waste energy. When you seek money or power for the sake of the ego, you spend energy chasing the illusion of happiness instead of enjoying happiness in the moment. When you seek money for personal gain only, you cut off the flow of energy to yourself, and interfere with the expression of nature's intelligence. But when your actions are motivated by love, there is no waste of energy. When your actions are motivated by love, your energy multiplies and accumulates—and the surplus energy you gather and enjoy can be channeled to create anything that you want, including unlimited wealth.[1]

Recently, I was trying to make a decision about how to handle a situation in which I felt treated unjustly by someone. I thought I had made some progress because of my willingness to take responsibility for how I had helped create the situation. I knew that I was still in my thought system, however, because I wanted to confront this person, tell him how I felt, and let him know I was going to make sure I did not invite unjust treatment anymore. This decision did not create good feelings.

---

1. Deepak Chopra, *The Seven Laws of Spiritual Success* (San Rafael: Amber-Allen Publishing & New World Library, 1994).

I decided to get quiet and meditate for a while. The understanding that I was in my thought system allowed me to dismiss the thoughts and listen for wisdom from my heart. It didn't take long for me to receive a message: *Are you going to use love power or anger power? Sharing your feelings from love will be much more effective than sharing them from anger. There will be no sense of blame. You will simply practice what you preach about identifying a problem and finding a solution. Taking responsibility is much more effective from love than from anger.*

Once again, I had seen how easy it is to make rules out of wisdom. I had seen the wisdom of taking responsibility for how I contribute to situations. In this situation, I was doing this as a rule, and it didn't help me feel better. As soon as I used my feelings compass to find that I was in my thought system, I was open for fresh inspiration from my heart.

When I talked with my friend, I was able to state the problem without any emotional attachment. I simply said, "This is a problem, and I know we can find a solution." And we did because he did not feel defensive, as he most likely would have if I had attacked him.

A decision may make sense in one situation. If you make a rule out of it, however, you will lose touch with your inner wisdom and inspiration. No matter how similar the situation is, it may call for a completely different decision at another time. Only your inner wisdom can let you know.

INTELLIGENCE

Joe commented to Zeke, "I'd rather be smart and miserable than a happy fool."

Wise old Zeke asked, "Is that smart?"

Some people believe that it is a sign of intelligence to find fault and ugliness in the world; they call it being realistic and think that anyone who can't see the negativity as they do is being a blind fool. Of course, these people are not happy when they are being negative.

I prefer a definition of intelligence that includes the wisdom to be happy, no matter what other people think.

PATIENCE

"I just lost my patience," claimed Helen.

"If only I could be more patient," sighed Henry.

And so the struggle goes when people believe that patience is a matter of self-control or a quality that must be developed. Patience is natural when you experience life through your heart and feel full of peace and contentment.

Impatience is created from thoughts of dissatisfaction, expectation, or judgment. Dismiss those thoughts and you have patience because it is impossible to feel impatient and satisfied at the same time.

You may ask, "How can I possibly be patient when someone is doing something I know they shouldn't be doing?" Turning the other cheek always seemed terribly wimpy to me. It makes sense now. When we see the innocence in what others do from a lack of understanding about the dynamics of their thought system, it makes no sense to lash out at them or to lose our own peace of mind in reaction to their insecurity. It does make sense to create a loving, forgiving atmosphere in which they can best gain understanding or to know when they are not ready to learn.

FORGIVENESS

An unwillingness to forgive is one of the greatest blocks to inner wisdom. It is based on ego, judgments, self-righteousness, lack of compassion, and a belief that there is only one possible reality—mine!

The ego has some very powerful hooks. Being "right" is a huge one. For many of us, being right wins over love and peace most of the time. Being right can take many forms. Sometimes we feel that we have a *right* to feel miserable. After all, look what those people (our parents) or that person (boss, spouse, friend) did to us. "I would much rather feel miserable about that than to let it go and feel love and peace. That would mean I would have to let go of all my judgments and feel compassion—and (gulp) even forgiveness." There is only one thing to be gained by not forgiving—misery!

> Forgiveness is natural from a level of consciousness that includes compassion, love, humor, gratitude, and peace of mind.

People who have the popular opinion that forgiveness is something you have to work at or try to do are engrossed in ego and judgment. It is self-righteous to think, "Well, I know you did something wrong, but I will be big enough to forgive you." Or, "You did a despicable thing, and you don't deserve forgiveness." Lack of forgiveness harms the unforgiving more than the unforgiven. It is impossible to be happy while holding on to judgments.

Anyone who says, "I will forgive, but I won't forget," doesn't understand forgiveness: Forgiveness *is* forgetting. It is realizing that ego, expectations, and judgments are thoughts that are not worth hanging on to, and, when we let go of them, they are forgotten. Dismissing negative thoughts and forgiving are synonymous.

Forgiveness is natural from a level of consciousness that includes compassion, love, humor, gratitude, and peace of mind. Forgiveness is not even an issue when we have these feelings because when we see with *understanding*, there is nothing to forgive.

CIRCUMSTANCES

Contrary to popular opinion, circumstances have nothing to do with happiness. As we have discussed, our thoughts about circumstances create our state of mind.

We often hear people say things like "I'll be happy when I finish school"; ". . . when I'm married"; ". . . when I'm single"; ". . . when I have more money"; ". . . when I have children"; or ". . . when you do what I want you to do."

If you are not happy before you get what you want, you won't be happy after you get it. People who think they are happy when they first get what they want find that happiness doesn't last long. When things settle down, they feel that old, nagging insecurity and dissatisfaction or get trapped back in their feelings of unhappiness the first time things don't go the way they think they should have.

During a discussion of these principles, one man asked, "Do you mean to tell me that losing my legs would not be a reason for me to be unhappy?"

He was told, "That is right. It is only what you could think about losing your legs that could create unhappiness."

He replied, "That is the most stupid thing I ever heard of."

Another man who was listening spoke up, "It is true. I lost both my legs in Vietnam, but I have never been happier. That does not mean I don't wish I had my legs. I would love to have my legs back, but

> The most helpful thing is to accept yourself and have compassion for yourself as you are—without judgment.

before I learned about these principles, I didn't know how to be happy when I had them. Now I know how to be happy even without them."

Happiness is a state of mind that allows you to see things differently. In a happy state of mind (from your heart), you will see life with gratitude and a different perspective. Circumstances look different when seen through the filter of your thought system.

Happiness is a state of mind that comes from *within*.

You may be wondering, "But what about things that are beyond my control, like sickness or negative things other people do?" When you have peace of mind and contentment, you will see *what is* without judgment, like the wise man in the following story.

A HORSE STORY

Many years ago, a wise man lived in an old mountain village. One day a beautiful, wild stallion ran into his corral. When the villagers heard the news, they came to his farm and marveled, "What a wonderful thing! You are so fortunate!"

The wise man replied, "Maybe so, maybe not."

A few days later, the stallion broke the corral fence and ran away. When the villagers heard the news, they came to his farm and said, "What a terrible thing! What bad luck!"

The wise man replied, "Maybe so, maybe not."

The next day, the stallion returned, bringing a whole herd of mares. When the villagers heard the news, they came and exclaimed, "Now you are the richest man in the village, and surely the luckiest!"

The wise man replied, "Maybe so, maybe not."

The wise man's son tried to break one of the mares but was thrown and broke his leg. When the villagers heard the news, they came and sympathized, "What a tragedy! Who will help you now with the harvest? This is such a misfortune!"

The wise man replied, "Maybe so, maybe not."

The next day, the Cossacks came to get all the young men of the village to fight in their wars. They did not take the wise man's son because of his broken leg.

SEEING *WHAT IS* WITHOUT JUDGMENT

You may ask, "But what if I'm not in a state of mind that allows me to see things without judgment? What if I do have negative thoughts and feelings about external circumstances?"

The most helpful thing is to accept yourself and have compassion for yourself as you are—without judgment. Of course this can be difficult because when your state of mind comes from your thought system, it is difficult to have compassion even for yourself. This is why it can be helpful to get quiet and just wait for it to pass. Knowledge of the four principles may help you do at least that much. Knowing it will pass, even when you feel stuck, is the first step toward getting unstuck.

When you are confronted with circumstances that you can't seem to understand and you add negative thoughts to them, you have two things to make you miserable: the circumstances and your negative thoughts about them. Your thoughts are usually much worse than the circumstances, and it is your thoughts that produce your feelings.

You don't see the beauty of life or experience feelings of joy and gratitude when you waste time and energy on judgments. Judgments fill you with toxic feelings.

A good example is the story of two men who lost their fortunes. One was distraught about his circumstances and jumped off a tall building. The other man saw them as an opportunity to start over again in something new. (As you might expect, the man who jumped off the building was not a happy person even when he had his fortune, whereas the man who saw the opportunity had been enjoying life during all his varied circumstances.)

Some argue, "I can understand how that applies to most circumstances, but not to others." People will often think of extreme cases to prove a principle invalid instead of simply applying the principle to situations in their own lives, where they would know it is true.

I have found that as I experience the principles in areas where I do not doubt, my understanding deepens. I then doubt less and see the principles in areas I had formerly been unable to understand. This is a progression that never ends. Understanding keeps deepening, and life keeps appearing more beautiful. Actually, life *is* always beautiful. We either see it or we don't.

CHAPTER TWELVE

Detours

There are many detours that keep you from accessing the natural good feelings and wisdom of your heart. All these detours come from the old perceptions and beliefs that have formed your programmed thought system.

INSECURITY

Even though insecurity is just another thought, it can be very powerful when taken seriously. Every negative act is based on thoughts that produce insecurity. In other words, if someone says or does something that hurts you, it is because of their insecurity. (Of course, you wouldn't be hurt if you listened from your heart instead of from your thought system.) The insecurity may be at a subconscious level, but it is followed by each individual's interpretations of what he or she needs to do to compensate. Thought-provoked insecurity may appear in the form of aggressiveness, shyness, drug abuse, self-righteousness, selfishness, the need to prove one's worth through achievements, feelings of inadequacy, and any other negative act you can think of.

Many positive acts also are motivated by insecurity from the thought system. "Pleasers" ("approval junkies") do loving things for others to "buy" love. Powermongers may engage in positive actions to serve their purposes. (I won't even go into politics.) From your heart, you won't judge these acts; you will *understand*.

Insecurity may lead some people to adopt the belief system of someone else or to imagine that others are the source of their wisdom. This is especially dangerous when they follow a guru or religious leader because they hear beautiful words of wisdom and don't listen to their own inner wisdom. This is not the intention of many gurus or religious leaders. They keep telling their followers that the truth is within. Other so-called gurus gather followers to form cults. People would not be led astray if they listened to their inner wisdom.

The teen years often present a vulnerable time because adolescents want so much to "fit in." And when teenagers cave in to peer pressure, they relinquish their ability to listen to their inner wisdom. What a difference it could make for them to *understand* the four principles.

EGO AND SELF-IMPORTANCE

The illusion of insecurity is strongly connected with the illusions of ego and proving self-importance. It is impossible to find happiness through trying to prove self-importance. Temporary relief might be found through some kind of achievement, but it doesn't last.

When you get off track into your thought system, notice how often the detour is related to proving your self-importance. It is strenuous just to think about all the antics we go through in life to prove something that has no need to be proven. Your worth (or the worth of anyone) is not an issue when you see yourself and others from your heart and spiritual source.

> You will find natural happiness when you recognize the ego for what it is and stop taking it seriously.

The ego is the strongest part of the thought system. It works very hard to protect itself. It is not at all interested in being dismissed and replaced by your spiritual source. However, you will feel like a different person when you don't take your ego seriously.

I used to scoff at the question "Who am I?" Now the question makes sense because I realize I am different when experiencing life through my heart than I am when experiencing life through my thought system and ego.

We all created our egos subconsciously when we were very young and thought that we needed to prove ourselves to be worthy of love. It actually may have served us well at the time in dealing with people who were functioning from their own programmed thought system and provided conditional love (even when that was not their intention). Over time, the ego becomes more master than servant. While coming from your thought system, you fail to notice that your self-created ego is no longer useful or helpful. You will find natural happiness when you recognize the ego for what it is and stop taking it seriously. Then you have access to the inner wisdom from your heart that truly serves you. You will know you have nothing to prove. Instead you can enjoy *being*.

I know that much of what I say is repetitious. The principles are truly simple, but the thought system refuses to acknowledge the simplicity. Forgive me if I assume that you might be having the same difficulty that I and others had while trying to understand these concepts. As I said before, hearing the same thing over and over just might be the only way to undo the old conditioning of your thought system. I can almost hear those who are still struggling object: "Isn't that selfish to sit around like a blob enjoying yourself?" *Being* who you truly are when you are no longer a prisoner of your thought system does not mean you will sit around like a selfish blob. It means that what you do will be inspired from your heart. Your actions will not be contaminated or driven by past misperceptions that created your ego.

> The power of love from the heart is the only force that can overcome the effects of insecurity in the world.

The fun thing about the ego is that every time you recognize it for what it is, you can't help laughing about it, thus causing it to lose its power. Your ego loves catching you off guard, however, so that it can sneak back. By keeping the principles in mind, you can play hide-and-seek with your ego.

IT IS SO EASY TO SEE IN OTHERS

Have you ever noticed how easy it is to observe illusionary ego beliefs in others and how difficult it is to maintain that perspective with yourself? The thought systems and egos of characters in movies and novels become very obvious when observed through an *understanding* of the four principles. Life can be nicer when you have as much fun catching your own ego and observing your own thought system.

Like other illusions, insecurity loses its power once you know what it is. *Understanding* inspires love and compassion for yourself as well as for others who may not know that their negative behavior is based on the illusions and insecurities of the thought system. The power of love from the heart is the only force that can overcome the effects of insecurity in the world.

JUDGMENTS

Many excuse their judgment of others by calling it "righteous" judgment. Righteous judgment is rare; because it is based on feelings of love and understanding, it leaves no negative feelings in its wake. Instead, the results of righteous judgment are positive. Abhorring child abuse is an example of righteous judgment when it is followed by actions to protect children and educate the parents out of love and compassion instead of self-righteousness.

"I'm telling you this for your own good" is not an example of righteous judgment but of taking your own separate reality seriously and thinking that it is the "right" reality. Self-righteous judgment of others is not helpful; it leaves negative feelings. When you dismiss your thought system, you rise to a higher level of consciousness where judgments are replaced with love, compassion, and inspiration.

Debra was having negative feelings about her friend Georgia, who was living her life in ways that "looked negative" to Debra. Debra decided to stay away from her for a while, which could have been a reasonable solution if Debra had simply stayed away without passing judgment on Georgia or herself. Debra contaminated her decision, however, by judging herself: "If I were a bigger person, I wouldn't let her behavior bother me. I should be more loving and understanding." Debra's self-judgments kept her in a low mood, limited her perspective, and produced more judgments of her friend.

She judged Georgia, too: "She is being so self-centered, self-righteous, manipulative, and self-serving. She thinks her reality is the only valid one in the world." Debra was able to find several others who had the same judgments about Georgia, which seemed to justify her own thoughts. (The ego loves validation, and you can always find plenty of others whose ego will join yours in thinking you are "right.")

Debra lived in an anxious state of mind as she continued the vicious cycle of self-condemnation and judgment of Georgia. Finally, she used her feelings as a compass and could see her judgments for the thoughts they were. Debra decided to get quiet and look for the gift (or lesson) in this situation.

Being without judgment is being in a state of humility and quiet. During the "quiet," Debra's understanding deepened. She had a mirror insight: She *saw* that she often did all the same "selfish" things that she attributed to Georgia. She saw that her judgments about Georgia were "self-centered, self-righteous, manipulative, and self-serving." It had been easier to see these "faults" in Georgia because they seemed worse than her own. From her inner wisdom, Debra realized that what she saw in Georgia was only a reflection of her own behavior, even though it wasn't "as bad."

Debra and Georgia are now great friends. Debra sees all Georgia's actions as endearing—or looks in the mirror at her own reflection if anything starts to bother her. These mirror insights help her *see* her own thought system at work. She can then see the humor, drop the thoughts, and enjoy her natural good feelings.

In his lectures, Wayne Dyer often gives the analogy of an orange to make the point that what we see comes from inside us. When you squeeze an orange, you get orange juice because that is what is inside the orange. When humans get "squeezed" (challenged), what they see in others can be seen only if it is inside themselves. If you look closely, you will always find the trait inside yourself that you are judging in another. Of course, you won't think your trait is as bad. In fact, you may feel better about yourself because you think someone else is worse. Rudolf Dreikurs used to call this *deflating another in order to inflate oneself.* Others have given the example of three fingers pointing back at you whenever you point a finger at someone else. These analogies simply point out the need for compassion instead of judgment—for yourself and others. It doesn't mean you should work on your own faults. That is another concept of the thought system. Again, when coming from your heart and spiritual source, there is nothing to work on. Being isn't work. It is fun or just plain peaceful.

STEREOTYPING

Another danger of judgment is that we often characterize people by what they do from their thought system and decide that this is the sum total of who they are. Often we dismiss what they do from their heart as "just an act." In so doing, we have taken the detour of believing in the reality of the thought system instead of the reality of the heart. We are more willing to trust the validity of behavior from a low mood than behavior from a high mood. This is mischievous behavior from the ego, trying to convince us that *we* are better if others seem worse.

It would be a topsy-turvy concept to stereotype people when they are functioning from their hearts instead of from their thought systems. Yet that is who they really are.

JUDGMENTS FROM OTHERS

With *understanding*, you will pay no more attention to the judgments of others than to your own. You will see that you get into enough trouble taking your own judgments seriously and that "shoulds" and "shouldn'ts" are no more helpful from others than they are from yourself.

Virginia dreaded being around her mother for long because she felt intimidated by her judgments, which she reacted to with rebellion. Her mother reacted to Virginia's rebellion with more judgments.

After learning about the principles, Virginia spent a delightful four days traveling across the country with her mother. As Virginia tells the story, "Every time my mom came out with what I used to call a judgment, I just saw it as her reality. Instead of rebelling and letting her know that I thought what she thought was stupid, I saw it as interesting. I could even see the insecurity behind her so-called judgments and feel compassion for her. I still didn't agree with her on everything, but I respected her right to see things differently. I was also able to respect my own way of seeing things without getting huffy about it. We had a great time. We talked and shared more than we have in my whole life."

LIVING FOR—OR AGAINST—SOMEONE ELSE

Too many people take the detour of trying to live up to the expectations of others and become "pleasers," or "approval junkies." By doing so, they discount their own inner wisdom and inspiration. Others take the detour of rebelling against the expectations of others, even when following their suggestions might be to their benefit. It is easy to understand why and how people create these decisions when we look at their childhood conditioning about the need to live up to the expectations of parents and teachers or to rebel against them.

> People talk about self-esteem as though it is something we have or don't have on a permanent basis—and that we can "give" it to children. This is a myth that is perpetuated continuously.

When we are little, the approval of others is very important to us. We form all kinds of beliefs about what we need to do to get approval and how to protect ourselves when we don't.

Once there was a little girl named Marie who went to visit her aunt and uncle, where she learned how to make bread. Her aunt and uncle thought that was wonderful and praised her and told her over and over how much they appreciated her bread.

Marie went home and baked bread for her family. No one said anything about her bread but just ate it. Marie decided she would never make bread for her family again because they didn't appreciate it and praise her.

Then one day she discovered that she enjoyed making bread for the fun of it. She loved getting her hands into the dough to knead it; she loved the aroma of the baking bread; and she especially loved eating it hot out of the oven, dripping with butter and sometimes honey. She also loved sharing it with anyone who wanted to have some. She realized that when she was living for or against someone else, she didn't taste the bread.

SELF-ESTEEM

Have you noticed that self-esteem (as defined by the world) is very elusive? One minute you have it and the next you don't—depending on what you do or what others think. When you do something well or someone praises you, you feel good (have self-esteem). However, when you don't do well or when someone criticizes you, your self-esteem disappears. Yet people talk about self-esteem as though it is something we have or don't have on a permanent basis—and that we can "give" it to children. This is a myth that is perpetuated continuously.

The truth is that self-esteem is a moment-to-moment state of mind. When you are listening to your inner wisdom, you have it, but when you are dependent on the approval of others or following false notions from the thought system, you don't. Self-esteem is one of the natural good feelings inherent in every human being when living from the heart. You have self-esteem when you esteem yourself enough to listen to the messages from your heart.

An extremely popular detour is the one of "working on" self-esteem. Since lack of self-esteem is an illusion that exists only in the thought system, it makes no sense to give the illusion credibility by trying to *attain* self-esteem. Focusing on self-esteem is a detour guaranteed to lead you away from your natural, inherent self-esteem. As with happiness, you can't find self-esteem by looking for it. You have inherent and natural self-esteem and happiness when you dismiss the thought system that keeps them buried.

ANGER

It takes little to take us down the "big A" detour when our thought system is in control. We may get angry when people don't drive the way we want them to or when others don't respond as we want them to at exactly the moment we want them to (preferably by reading our mind). We may get angry when equipment doesn't work the way we want it to or when a retail clerk doesn't behave as though we are the most important customer in the store. We get especially angry when someone else gets angry at us. I'm sure you could add to this list.

It is important to remember that all negative reactions are based on subconsciously stored thoughts and beliefs. As the *Course in Miracles* teaches in lesson 5, "I am never upset for the reason I think."[1] Lesson 7 teaches, "I see only the past."[2] This is an excellent description of the thought system. Everything we see from our thought system is seen through the filters of our past. When we do not *understand* these perception prisons, we are blocked from our ability to see with fresh perspective from our inner wisdom.

---

1. *A Course in Miracles: Workbook For Students* (Huntington Station, New York: The Foundation for Inner Peace), p. 8.
2. Ibid, p. 11.

When we see our anger as reality, we have different ways of expressing it. Sometimes we verbalize anger, sometimes we sulk, and sometimes we have a silent tantrum against ourselves and get depressed. We miss so much of the beauty of life when we take this detour.

Another common detour is the belief that there are certain things that justify anger. It is normal to feel angry when we have been violated in any way. However, maintained anger over this or any other immoral act does not solve anything; it just makes us feel bad and keeps us from enjoying life *now* or from accessing our inner wisdom to know what to do.

One therapist worked in group-therapy sessions with sixty women who were victims of rape or incest. For many years these women talked about their anger, beat on pillows, and yelled and screamed about their anger. They spent hours confirming that what had happened to them in the past was the reason they could not hold jobs, were alcoholics, and could not participate in lasting relationships.

After the therapist learned about the four principles, she apologized to the women in her groups: "I'm sorry, ladies, but I have been doing it all wrong. From now on we will no longer dwell on the past but will talk about some principles that will teach you how to have happiness and peace of mind in life now."

A few women dropped out because they did not want to give up their anger. The remaining women soon learned to enjoy life when they stopped living in the past through their thought system. A two-year follow-up showed that they maintained their good feelings and were successful in their jobs and relationships. Some were training to become therapists or educators so that they could share what they had learned.

> Stored anger based on past perceptions and beliefs can fester into physical disease, and it can destroy relationships.

One woman appeared on a panel with other rape victims. She was obviously a very happy person. The moderator of the panel questioned her, "Don't you feel angry? Hasn't your rape experience affected your relationship with men? Why are you so happy?"

"That experience took up eleven minutes of my life," she answered. "I don't intend to give it one more second in my thoughts. Life is so full of good things to enjoy, why should I waste time thinking about the past?"

When you don't like what happened in the past, it doesn't make sense to keep re-creating it in your thoughts and then multiplying the unhappiness by adding anger. Your anger has a message for you. Anger turns into resentment when you miss the message but keep the messenger. Try the methods of quieting discussed in chapter 10. Be gentle with yourself and listen to your heart. Like all negative thoughts, anger loses its power when seen with *understanding*. From your heart, you will know what to do.

There is a popular opinion that if you don't get your anger out, you will store it and it will fester. This can be true when you are living from your thought system. Stored anger based on past perceptions and beliefs can fester into physical disease, and it can destroy relationships. Biofeedback research suggests that one moment of thought-provoked anger substantially suppresses the immune system for eight hours. Other research demonstrates the healing effectiveness of the natural good feelings from the heart.

Obviously, it is not a good idea to store anger. The key is *how* to get it out. One way is to *understand* the thinking ability that created the thoughts that led to anger and then dismiss it. Another way is to share how you feel (not how someone else has "made" you feel) in a way that invites clarification of separate realities. What you do is not as important as the state of mind behind what you do. Sharing how you feel from your heart is very different from sharing your feelings from your thought system.

Another way to get anger out (literally) is to look for the lesson, or gift. We have already discussed how "looking in the mirror" for reflections of yourself can lead to *understanding* as you see the message or the life lesson. Seeing the message often leads to forgiveness.

Forgiveness transforms anger. Forgiveness is automatic when you see others or circumstances from your heart. The heart sees innocence. The heart feels compassion. The heart *understands*. You may need to get quiet for a while before you see through the eyes of your heart.

Sometimes it takes a healing process to expose the subconscious thought or belief behind anger, hurt, or any other debilitating emotion. An important part of healing is "walking in another person's shoes. . . . Go into that person's head to understand and identify their thoughts and feelings and intentions."[3] This helps one to truly understand separate realities and see with understanding, compassion, and forgiveness. Healing can be so complete that old beliefs and decisions from the past are gone.

THE PAST

Another popular detour is into the past. The past cannot exist unless we think about it, yet many live their whole lives on this detour.

Through brain research, it has been discovered that our brains are storage containers for every thing in our pasts. Wilder Penfield[4] found that he could probe any part of the brain and the patient would remember the details of specific events from the past, including smells and feelings: "When Penfield and Jasper considered their results, it appeared that the brain held an untold number of film clips, each with sound and picture, of vivid events from the patient's past. The replaying would evoke, as well, the emotions that accompanied the original experiences."[5]

The brain also stores our interpretations of past events even though they are not correct. The thought system turns these interpretations into beliefs that act as filters to keep us from seeing the truth in the moment.

3. Valerie Seeman Moreton, N.D., *Heal the Cause* (San Diego: Kalos Publishing, 1996), p. 339.
4. Jefferson Lewis, *Something Hidden: A Biography of Wilder Penfield* (Garden City, New York: Doubleday & Company, Inc., 1981), p. 201.
5. Lewis, p. 198.

For example, as a child you may have decided you were unlovable or inadequate. This decision was not made based on the truth. Your parents may have reprimanded you because they believed that this was the best way to show their love. They may have been too busy *doing* to give you the attention you wanted. The truth did not matter as much as your *interpretation* of the situation, which was cemented into a belief. This belief now may act as a filter to keep you from accepting love in the present. *Understanding* can eliminate the belief. When you *see* and interpret an event differently, from your heart, your feelings and decisions will also change.

Linda had an experience in her past in which it seemed to her that her father was embarrassed to hug her. She assumed he didn't love her, which she interpreted to mean that she was not lovable. If she was not lovable to her own father, then she must not be lovable to anyone. She constantly tried to prove that she was worthy of love, but because her behavior was based on insecurity, she acted demanding and unlovable. She went to a therapist who tried to help her "get in touch with her anger at her father." In her heart, this did not feel right to Linda. Years later she found a therapist who taught her the four principles.

> When you understand that the past exists only when you think about it and that it is only your interpretation of what happened, it becomes difficult to take your thoughts about the past seriously.

Understanding helped Linda dismiss her thought system. Inspiration from her heart helped her see that her father felt uncomfortable hugging not because he didn't love her but because he had never received affection himself. She had another healing insight: She knew that even if her father had *not* loved her, that would have been a consequence of his thought system, not an indication that she was unworthy of being loved.

Three sisters got together at a family reunion and began discussing the past. Each had perceptions of events that had a profound impact on the decisions they had made about themselves. However, when each shared her memory, the other two sisters were surprised at the interpretation. All of them had been present at each event, yet each had experienced them very differently. Which perception of each memory was *the truth*? The past is not the truth. The past is only your perception of the truth.

When you understand that the past exists only when you think about it and that it is only your interpretation of what happened, it becomes difficult to take your thoughts about the past seriously. In the same way, when you see the innocence of others' past actions, knowing that they did the best they could from their level of understanding at the time, you will feel differently about those actions.

Paula often complained about all the terrible things her mother had done and said to her in the past. A therapist asked her, "Do you think your mother stayed up late at night plotting ways to make your life miserable?"

With reluctance, Paula admitted, "No."

A week later Paula said that that question had helped her understand the principle of separate realities and led her out of her thought system to her heart, where she felt compassion and forgiveness. It had become clear to her that her mother really did love her and had done the best she could, considering her own insecurities.

Paula added that her inner wisdom then led her to "look in the mirror" and see how she was repeating many of the same behaviors with her own son: "I punish him when he makes mistakes, even though I hated it when my mother did that. I can see now that she probably did it for the same reasons I do. I'm afraid that if I don't punish him, he won't learn to do better, and I want him to do better because I love him. But when I was a child, I can remember wishing my mother would understand how I felt and teach me with love instead of punishment."

Paula was able to forgive her mother and herself when she understood that the "mistakes" they had both made were simply the results of getting sidetracked from love and enjoyment of their children into thoughts that produced fear and insecurity.

LIGHTEN UP, KEEP IT SIMPLE, AND COME FROM LOVE

When I am miserably on my way down the path of low moods, I have usually taken three detours at once. First, I have taken my perceptions seriously (usually having to do with ego, expectations, and judgments). Second, I have then tried to analyze complicated ways to solve the problem. Finally, I have come from perceptions of insecurity that manifest themselves in anger or hopelessness. In other words, from this state of mind, all the possible, complicated solutions don't really seem like solutions at all but more like ways of seeking revenge or escape. What detours! As soon as I tune into my inner wisdom (sometimes in minutes, sometimes in days), I can see what I have done and feel inspired to lighten up, keep it simple, and come from love.

Lightening up usually involves raising your perspective so that you see the big picture. When you lighten up and quit taking things too seriously, what once seemed like a tragedy can be seen as an interesting event, as a stepping-stone rather than a stumbling block, as a great gift full of lessons to be learned, or perhaps simply as a humorous situation.

Keeping it simple usually means that the solution becomes obvious and uncomplicated when you drop your judgments that lead to anger, hatred, revenge, or self-pity. Trying to figure things out from your thought system is usually complicated; figuring things out from your heart (love) is simple.

Coming from love means that what you do is not as important as how you do it. For example, maybe it would be a wise thing to fire an employee or leave a relationship. This can be done with love and respect rather than with anger and revenge. When you are doing the obvious thing to handle a situation, there is no need for anger. Lighten up, keep it simple, and come from love.

IT GETS EASIER TO AVOID DETOURS

Even a limited understanding of the principles keeps you pointed in the right direction so that your understanding keeps getting deeper. The deeper the understanding, the easier it gets.

Let good feelings from your heart be your only guide to avoid detours, to enjoy the detours, or to find your way back home.

CHAPTER THIRTEEN

Relationships

There are many different kinds of relationships: spouses, children, parents, friends, animals, colleagues, bosses, employees, and drivers on the freeway. Some are closer than others. Have you ever noticed that those closest to you can often trigger the ego of your thought system easier than any other kind of relationship? Have you noticed how much easier it can be to share wisdom with friends who are having relationship problems than to see it for yourself when you become emotionally involved? Why is that? Why is it sometimes easier to have empathy and show more respect for others than it is to those closest to you? And why is it sometimes easier to give unconditional love to an animal than to a person?

The answers to all these questions are directly related to your thought system. The last question provides the best analogy—animals don't challenge your thought system or your ego. You don't have unrealistic expectations of your pets, so they don't invite your judgments.

You don't expect an animal to be different. You don't get upset when an animal doesn't "agree" with you.

I'm not suggesting that you treat those you love like an animal (although I considered it) but to use this analogy as another way to help you understand the power of the thought system to cause problems. The four principles can show you where problems originate in any relationship. They can show you why those closest to you can be the most challenging to your thought system.

1. Trying to change the reality of another person—that is, fighting over who is right instead of respecting differences and finding them interesting.

2. Getting caught up in negative thoughts—judgments, interpretations, the past, proving ego and self-importance, and other forms of thought-produced insecurity—which happens when you focus on the content of your thoughts instead of realizing that thinking is a function.

3. Not dismissing negative thoughts (or at least not getting quiet) during low moods or low levels of consciousness but instead trying to discuss them, figure them out, or solve them.

4. Sharing negative feelings that come from the insecurity of your thought systems, with the belief that another person should understand them, take them seriously, and adopt them as their own reality, instead of using your feelings compass to let you know where you are.

When you don't understand these principles, you may react from the fears and old beliefs of your thought system instead of acting from the love of your heart and inner wisdom.

SEPARATE REALITIES RELATING TO RELATIONSHIPS

Amy and Sean had daily arguments. No matter what the subject, the theme was always the same.

Amy: "You have to be blind as a bat not to see things my way!"

Sean: "If you had any brains at all, you would know that *my* way is right!"

Amy and Sean are stuck in the illusions of their separate realities.

Have you ever tried to convince your partner (or child) that your point of view was the right one and felt as if you were talking to a wall? You were actually talking to two walls: the wall of your own unique reality and the wall of your partner's unique reality. (Literally talking to a wall could be easier because a wall does not have its own point of view, and you wouldn't have any expectations from a wall.) It is even less productive to try convincing your partner, who already knows

> When you dismiss your judgments and expectations, you see a very different and interesting person in front of you.

how things are and would like to convince you. Your partner is usually seeing his or her reality with as much inner wisdom as you are seeing yours: zero.

Jeannette strongly believed her children needed lots of rules and guidance; Duane believed he should sacrifice anything important to him in order to cater to their whims. Duane thought Jeannette was a tyrant; Jeannette thought Duane was a wimp. Both were so entrenched in their separate realities that they could not access their inner wisdom. Sometimes wisdom might take the form of guidance, sometimes the form of doing things with or for others. In either case, guidance or doing things for others based on good feelings and inspiration from their hearts will be different from those actions based on self-righteousness, defensiveness, or judgment from their thought systems.

When you take your reality seriously, it becomes an illusionary frame of reference—or a distorted pair of glasses. You don't realize how those glasses distort and filter everything in your world. When you dismiss your judgments and expectations, you see a very different and interesting person in front of you.

Dorene and Charles were experiencing marital difficulty because they were deeply enmeshed in their separate realities. Their distorted frames of reference prevented them from seeing anything with love and compassion.

Dorene complained about being third or fourth priority in Charles's life. From this belief, she felt hurt. As many of us do, she covered her hurt feelings with anger, which she expressed by blaming and attacking Charles for not putting her first.

Charles took her attacks seriously and generated feelings of inadequacy and defensiveness, which he expressed by acting disdainful toward Dorene. Charles's frame of reference included a belief that women were unfair and unreasonable anyway.

During her childhood, Dorene had had an experience that she had interpreted to mean that she was unimportant. She turned this interpretation into a belief that distorted every experience she had from then on. Subconsciously, she spent her life looking for evidence to support her belief in her unimportance, and she was so intent on this task that she missed any evidence that might change her belief.

This was obvious when she told the story of how she and Charles met and got married. Charles was dating Adele but quit seeing her and soon asked Dorene to marry him. Dorene did not see this as evidence that she was important to Charles. What she did notice was Adele's name on the wedding invitation list, which she saw as evidence that Adele was more important to him than she was. Charles's attempts to explain that he simply liked Adele as a friend fell on deaf ears.

Charles, in turn, had once had a childhood experience that he had interpreted to mean that women were unfair and unreasonable. He adopted this as such a strong belief that he was unaware of how he set women up to prove that he was right. In this case, he knew Dorene would probably be upset if he put Adele's name on the list, but, although it wasn't important to have Adele as a wedding guest, he wanted to be able to prove he was right about how unreasonable women can be. Of course, he claimed it was important because he had to justify his position.

You and I have enough perspective (because we are removed) to see the humor in the emotions and dramas they created by their thinking, but Dorene and Charles were not laughing. When we take the filters from our thought system seriously, it is impossible to see the situation with perspective.

Dorene and Charles were focused on what they were looking for through the filters of their thought systems, which left little time to share good feelings. When our attention is focused on looking for evidence to support our distorted beliefs, we miss the obvious, wonderful things going on around us.

We can always create what we are looking for. For example, if we believe that we will be rejected, we will act in such a way that invites rejection, or we will see rejection even in innocent behaviors.

After hearing about the four principles, Dorene and Charles finally dismissed their thoughts and saw each other very differently. They stopped "playing detective,"

> True acceptance is unconditional and allows us to see others with compassion, gratitude, and love.

looking for evidence to support their insecurities, and started seeing things from their hearts instead of their heads. Charles felt like reassuring Dorene that she was important, and Dorene felt like reassuring Charles that she trusted him. Neither one really needed reassurance any more, but each appreciated the loving gestures. They had learned to laugh at their silly thoughts and see the beauty of life and of each other.

ACCEPTANCE

A marriage counselor suggested to Hazel that she stop trying to change her husband and accept him the way he was. Three months later, Hazel complained, "But I *have* accepted him for three whole months, and he hasn't changed a bit!" Would you say that Hazel's idea of acceptance was conditional?

Acceptance is *understanding* that everyone has a separate reality. Acceptance means respecting differences, not conditional acceptance while expecting changes. Even though it is impossible to change other people's realities (only they can do that by changing their own thoughts), we often keep trying. True acceptance is unconditional and allows us to see others with compassion, gratitude, and love.

THOUGHTS AND MOODS
RELATING TO RELATIONSHIPS

Mary thought that Jim was not paying enough attention to her. When she self-righteously shared this with her friends, they told her the importance of letting him know how she felt. Mary decided that was a good idea, so that night when Jim sat down on the couch and started to read the newspaper, she sat next to him and said, "How come the newspaper is more important to you than I am?"

Jim defensively retorted, "Because the newspaper doesn't hassle me."

Mary ran to the bedroom and cried, and for the rest of the evening she did not speak to Jim. The next day she told all her friends that Jim had admitted he preferred the newspaper to her, so she might as well get a divorce.

Fortunately, Mary had an opportunity to learn about the principles. She dismissed the notions of insecurity from her thought system and was amazed how much her feelings about herself and Jim changed when she saw the world from her heart.

The next time Jim sat down to read the newspaper, she sat quietly next to him, feeling gratitude for having such a nice man for a husband. She could see past his defensive behavior and felt unconditional love because she had dismissed her own insecurities, judgments, and expectations.

Soon Jim put down the newspaper and gruffly asked, "Did you want to talk?"

Mary could feel that he was still in a low mood and replied, "No, I was just enjoying your presence." Suspiciously, Jim continued to read the newspaper. For several weeks, Mary continued to enjoy just being with Jim, no matter what he did. She had discovered her own inner happiness and peace of mind and was not affected by outside circumstances.

One day Jim came into the kitchen while Mary was preparing dinner. She asked, "Did you want something?"

"No," he replied, "I just wanted to be with you."

Some people who hear this story think Mary acted like a wimp who decided to passively put up with a jerk.

> We create our world from our thoughts and actions. We reap what we sow.

But look at her results: she found serenity, saw the goodness beneath Jim's gruffness, and inspired him to experience his own heart. Unconditional love has the power to lead others to their heart center.

Another person might follow his or her wisdom to do something else. When living in the heart, there are infinite possibilities about what to do, but the feelings behind the doing will be the same—compassion, forgiveness, gratitude, and all the other feelings that are the essence of love.

We create our world from our thoughts and actions. We reap what we sow: When we put negativity out into the world, we get negativity back. Yet when negativity comes back, most people forget that they put it out in the first place; they don't take responsibility for its creation by their thoughts and subsequent actions. (Mary did not see that she helped create Jim's defensiveness and gruffness with her expectations and criticism.) In the same way, when we put love out into the world, love comes back. Joy and happiness are contagious.

Are you still arguing that sometimes negative circumstances come to you even when you did nothing to create them? The point is that even if you have no personal responsibility for causing certain events, your *thoughts about them* give you more trouble than the circumstances themselves.

Sue's husband had an affair, and she was so hurt that she wanted revenge. She went to an attorney and said, "I want to hurt him as much as he hurt me. I want to leave him with as little as possible financially and to limit his child visitation rights as much as possible. I will make sure the kids don't even want to see him."

Sue was too hurt and angry to see that it was her thoughts about this situation that made her miserable. Fortunately, she chose a wise attorney, who asked, "Do you really want to hurt him in the worst way possible?"

"Yes."

The attorney said, "Then go back and live with him for six months. Be the very best wife you can imagine: Be loving, compassionate, understanding, forgiving, affectionate, and fun. He will feel lucky and will start loving you very much. In six months you can start divorce proceedings, which will hurt him emotionally and financially."

Sue objected, "I couldn't stand to live with him for six more months."

"Well, then you must not really want to hurt him in the worst way possible."

"Oh, yes I do," Sue said. "I will do it."

Two years later, the attorney saw Sue walking down a street. He asked, "What happened? I thought you were going to come back for a divorce."

Sue replied, "Are you kidding? He is the most wonderful man in the world. I wouldn't even think of leaving him." She must have done such a good job acting loving that she soon forgot it was an act and started enjoying the good feelings. Good feelings are extremely contagious, creating more good feelings in people who come in contact with them.

When an understanding of the principles changes how you see things, everything and everyone in your world looks different. It may seem as though others have changed, but it is your thoughts, and thus your reality and your feelings that have changed. Others often respond to your feeling level. When you give love, you get love—not necessarily because others give it back to you but because love will emanate from within. Feeling love does not depend on anything or anyone else.

You may ask, "But what if I just don't feel loving, and I'm not willing to 'act' as Sue did?" Whenever you feel the need to ask what to do, it is helpful to do nothing except dismiss your thoughts, get quiet, and wait until you feel good enough to know from your inner wisdom what to do.

And if you don't feel ready, you don't feel ready. What is, is. To simply accept *what is* can be very calming.

Remember that sometimes awareness of the principles will change your mood instantly, and you will tap into your heart and inner wisdom. Other times you may see that focusing on the content of your thoughts is producing your negative feelings, but you won't feel totally better immediately. Those times are more like when you have the flu; you have a level of understanding that doesn't change your state of mind immediately, but it may lead you to quietly take care of yourself until your mood passes.

I realized this after an experience of being caught up in thinking that my reality was much better than my husband's. I really believed he was wrong, and since it seemed so real to me, I certainly had to tell him about it. (Have you ever noticed that when you think other people are "wrong," you feel compelled to inform them?)

My tirade lasted about five minutes before my miserable feelings alerted me to what I was doing. Although I immediately shut up, I still didn't feel much better; I simply saw enough to get quiet and quit spreading my negative emotions around. I started thinking, "I should apologize." But I didn't feel like apologizing, so I just stayed quiet.

> When you feel love, compassion, or interest rather than judgment or defensiveness, you are listening deeply.

I forget how long it took me to feel better because I stopped thinking about my negative emotions, but the next day when I was feeling love and gratitude for my husband, we talked about what had happened. Since I was then in a loving mood, it felt natural to apologize without feeling blame and guilt. Barry said that he was aware that my silence the day before was different from my old sulky silences that sent out vibrations of anger and blame. He said, "It was very nice."

Another time I became upset when my husband and I missed an opportunity to go on a trip with friends because he had a hunting trip planned. I had several negative thoughts that gave me some bad feelings. I knew I was caught up in my thought system, but I didn't get quiet. Instead, I asked Barry, "Would you like to hear my crazy thoughts?"

Barry replied good humoredly, "Sure. Go ahead."

I said, "Hunting is more important to you than I am."

Barry calmly replied, "You know that isn't true. I had this planned way ahead. I'll be more than happy to take a trip with you anytime we can find a mutually agreeable time."

I humorously admitted, "I know, but I used to get away with it."

In the past I actually believed that hunting was more important to him than I am. The important difference this time was that I accepted responsibility for my crazy thinking. Even though I felt disappointed, I couldn't take it as seriously as I did when I listened to my thought system—and so this time I couldn't use it for manipulative purposes.

My awareness of "doing my insecurity number" made it impossible for those feelings to have much power. It was not long before I could see that I didn't need a trip to be happy. I didn't even need to be more important than hunting to be happy.

Intellectual understanding does not change our feelings, but it can help us dismiss our thoughts, or at least take them less seriously, until we receive inspiration from our hearts.

LISTENING

True listening is forgetting about the details, hearing what another person is feeling, and knowing when those feelings are coming from thoughts of insecurity. You recognize the difference from your own feeling level. When you feel love, compassion, or interest rather than judgment or defensiveness, you are listening deeply. *Understanding* the four principles changes the experience of listening.

When your partner is upset or caught up in thought, that is the time to listen, not to talk. Analyzing does not help. Listening is quietly responding with love. When you are in that state of mind, your inspiration will let you know exactly how to express love and encouragement— eventually, if not immediately. It might be humor. It might be time alone. It might be a loving touch. It might be a quiet walk. It might be time to rest. It might be time for reflective listening. You will know.

Another way for couples to avoid low moods is to avoid the thought system by just having fun together.

HAVE FUN TOGETHER

Have you ever noticed that when you are having fun to-gether, you are not being judgmental, critical, or dissatis-fied? Having fun can act as a catalyst to take you out of your thought system. When you want to experience love and good feelings in your relationships, it makes sense to do things together that bring pleasure and enjoyment.

LIVE IN GRATITUDE

When you dismiss negative thoughts, you are left with feelings of gratitude and appreciation for all that life has to offer. It makes no sense to live in negativity when love is just a dropped thought away. When following the treasure map to happiness and peace of mind, the natural state of a relationship is to enjoy unconditional love.

CHAPTER FOURTEEN

Myths About Relationships

As the following myths are presented, reality as seen through your heart and inner wisdom is shown to be the opposite of what you may have been taught all your life.

MYTH NO. 1: LOVE IS BLIND

Love is not blind. When you are in love, you are not blinded by judgments, expectations, and other kinds of filters from your thought system. You see differences as interesting, or with understanding and compassion. What other people might see as faults in your beloved, you find endearing, you defend, or you brush off as unimportant.[1]

---

1. It is important to note that these attitudes also could come from the thought system based on seeing a person through filters of who we think they are rather than who they are. When this is true, we become disappointed when they don't live up to our expectations. When coming from our hearts, disappointment never follows.

Because Bob promised to call Nancy at 9:30 but didn't call until 11:00, she thought he was inconsiderate and uncaring—and told him so. Her feelings let her know that she was in her thought system. This *understanding* immediately took her to her heart, and she remembered that when they had fallen in love, she had been understanding and compassionate when he called later than promised. It became obvious to her that it wasn't the circumstances but her thoughts that upset her. Her judgments and anger were her defense mechanisms to cover up feelings of insecurity. From her heart, she felt secure and loving again.

When you look through your judgment glasses, you see differences or circumstances without love or compassion. The judgment blinder is so powerful that it can even change what was once seen as a virtue into a "fault."

Marilyn fell in love with Jordan and admired the calm way he drove a car, which made her feel safe and relaxed on rides with him. After they got married, however, she found that it often drove her crazy to ride with him because he was not aggressive enough and didn't take risks to pass slow cars.

Marilyn had also admired Jordan for his quiet, easygoing dependability; he had been in the same job for twelve years, and she could set her clock by his departure and arrival. With her judgment glasses on, however, she started seeing him as boring and lacking in ambition. During their courtship, she had loved his flexibility and willingness to go along with all her suggestions. But through her judgment blinders, she saw him as spineless and weak, without an original thought in his head.

Marilyn divorced Jordan and married Steve, who was aggressive, ambitious, and opinionated. At first Marilyn admired these "virtues" in Steve and felt lucky to be married to an exciting man who knew what he wanted and where he was going. She felt protected and taken care of. Later, however, she saw him as controlling and unyielding because he would not do what she wanted him to do, and instead of feeling protected, she felt dominated and not taken seriously.

Marilyn divorced Steve and married another man like Jordan. She is now in her seventh marriage because she does not see that she loses her good feelings and happiness every time she puts on her blinders of judgment and expectation. She believes she sees reality through her blinders. She is also looking for happiness outside herself and blames others when she doesn't find it there.

From her heart, Marilyn would not need to look for love outside herself. She would be loving.

This may sound very idealistic and altruistic, but loving is natural from your heart. It becomes idealistic and altruistic only when you think you *should* be loving from your thought system.

MYTH NO. 2: IT IS IMPORTANT TO BE COMPATIBLE

Dolores divorced Scott. Her explanation: "We just weren't compatible." A pervasive distortion of the meaning of compatibility is the notion that two people must have the same beliefs and interests to live together harmoniously.

When you understand the principle of separate realities, you can see that it is impossible for two people to be the same. Couples fooled into thinking they have the same interests and beliefs get into trouble when they later find what they thought was the same is not.

Dolores and Scott were delighted to discover that they both enjoyed tennis. They were already in love but saw their mutual interest in tennis as proof they were "compatible." The trouble started because Dolores liked to play more often than Scott did, and he thought she took it too seriously. Dolores assumed that anyone really interested in tennis would feel exactly the same way she did about it. Both felt cheated and misunderstood, and, since they were apparently not as compatible as they had thought, divorce was the only solution they could see.

> It is unimportant to be compatible in today's commonly (and narrowly) defined way; we don't need to have the same interests and beliefs. We have compatibility when we see differences with interest, respect, and love.

The true meaning of compatibility is having the ability to live together in harmony. We all have this ability because compatibility is a natural state when we dismiss negative thoughts and respect differences instead of judging them.

Lillian was feeling dissatisfied with Garth because she claimed they had nothing in common. She felt that they would both be better off if they broke off their relationship and went their separate ways. Garth felt very hurt and lashed out, "You couldn't have a long-lasting re-lationship with anyone!"

Lillian replied indignantly, "How could you say such a stupid thing? I have had friends for years all over the country, even though we don't see each other often. And they are all deep friendships."

The next day Lillian saw a therapist who taught her about the four principles. Lillian felt good when she left the therapist's office, but a few hours later she started thinking again about what Garth had said. She felt the anger well up again. She decided to take the therapist's advice to get quiet and look for the message in the anger. It did not take long for her to receive an insight that made her laugh. She realized that she treated her friends with unconditional love and respect. She never criticized or judged or burdened them with her expectations. When they were down, she encouraged them; when they were up, she celebrated with them. Her love relation-ships started out the same way, but she would soon move away from her heart and into her head.

As soon as she realized this, she felt humbled. She was then able to drop her insecure thoughts, and start treating Garth the way she did her friends. Their love blossomed.

It is unimportant to be compatible in today's com-monly (and narrowly) defined way; we don't need to have the same interests and beliefs. We have compatibility when we see differences with interest, respect, and love. We are compatible when we share good feelings rather than judgments and expectations. We are naturally com-patible when we experience life through our hearts and inner wisdom rather than through our thought systems.

MYTH NO. 3: IT IS IMPORTANT TO COMMUNICATE ABOUT PROBLEMS

An overemphasis on the importance of communication in relationships is another pervasive distortion. How often have you heard someone say, "We just can't communicate" or "The key to a good relationship is communication"?

The distortion in these statements is the implied importance of making your partner understand and accept what you feel and what you believe. That is, if you can get your partner to believe your reality rather than his or her own, you have succeeded in "good" communication. This is the same as saying, "You should have my illusions, not your own."

No wonder so many are failing in their attempts at communication. It is impossible for your partner to believe your reality rather than his or her own. With *understanding*, you both might dismiss your realities for the illusions of thought that they are, but until then you would "rather fight than switch."

Because you are always communicating, either from your distorted thought system (fear) or from your heart (love), it is important to know where your communication is coming from. When you are communicating from your thought system, you are sharing negative feelings, thoughts, and beliefs. Even sulky or angry silences are a form of communication. When you are communicating from your heart, however, you are sharing the positive feelings that you experience through love, wisdom, and inspiration.

Sharing positive feelings is often done silently. Many couples rely more on quiet touching and less on verbal communication when they realize how inadequate words are to express beautiful feelings. When you are in a state of happiness and peace of mind, it is amazing how much you can enjoy what is usually referred to as mundane information. "Is dinner ready?" "I paid the bills today." "How are the kids?" "Shall we go to the beach?" Communication becomes light and easy, not heavy as it is when you communicate to "get it all out" or to make sure your partner knows how you feel (from your thought system).

This may sound boring to some people, but happiness and peace of mind are not boring. In that state of mind, it is common to feel so full of the joy of living and love for your partner that you are filled with gratitude.

You may wonder, "Does this mean we shouldn't talk about our separate realities?" What you do is not the point. Talking about your separate realities, or not talking about them, is simply a different experience when you understand the principles. It is not what you *do* that is important but rather the feeling behind what you do. With *understanding*, you will probably feel a sense of humor if you do talk about separate realties instead of taking them seriously.

MYTH NO. 4: NEVER GO TO SLEEP UNTIL YOU HAVE RESOLVED AN ARGUMENT

Sometimes the best way to dismiss thoughts of right and wrong is to set some kind of cooling-off period to help you get quiet. This could be done by sleeping it off, walking around the block, or doing something else that helps you feel better.

Kate and Frank believed that they should never go to sleep until they had resolved their arguments. They would stand toe to toe and argue about who was right and who was wrong. Since they were both caught up in their individual thought systems and separate realities, it was impossible to hear each other or solve anything. Since they believed they should be able to solve their arguments, their frustrations would build. Frank would finally leave, slamming the door behind him, and go to the nearest bar. Kate would go to bed but couldn't sleep because she was furiously thinking about their failure to solve the problem before going to sleep.

When they saw a therapist who taught them about the principles, they saw what they could do. Frank said to Kate, "Since I like to leave the house when I am upset, I will leave, but I won't slam the door, and I won't go to a bar. I'll take a walk around the block until my thought system is tucked away where it can't hurt me and I am able to enjoy how much I love you again. You can know that my leaving is not anger at you but just my recognition that I'm caught up in my negative thoughts and need to get quiet until they go away."

Kate said, "Since I enjoy relaxing in bed, I will do that. But instead of continuing to think about my negative thoughts, I will read a book or go to sleep with the reassuring knowledge that they are just thoughts. You can know I'm not going to bed to get away from you but to rest until the negative thoughts are gone and nothing is left but love."

MYTH NO. 5: A RELATIONSHIP WITHOUT FIGHTS IS SUPERFICIAL OR ONE-SIDED

Couples who understand the principles do not fight, or at least they realize that they are off track when they do. The peace between them does not mean that they are not going "deep enough" in their relationship or that one of them is surrendering too much. On the contrary, they respect each other instead of their programmed thought systems.

Sylvia said, "I can't remember the last time Tim and I had a fight. It has been at least four years. We had lots of fights before, but now we just enjoy each other."

"Lisa and I still have fights," said Scott, "but they are all silent. We know that if we feel like fighting, we are just in a low mood, or lost in our thought systems, so we keep quiet and wait for it to pass."

Beth said, "Tom and I used to have fights and lose respect for each other. We still have fights once in a while, but now we lose respect for the fights instead of for each other."

"When Dave and I have fights now," said Kathie, "we seldom take them seriously for long, so we end up laughing. It is especially fun to watch my 'Sarah Bernhardt act' while I am still taking things a little bit seriously."

I used to get upset when I wanted to "discuss" something with my husband, and he would tell me, "Forget it." I would retort, "What do you mean, 'forget it'? If you had any sensitivity at all, you would be upset too." Now I say, "Thanks for reminding me."

MYTH NO. 6: YOU'LL BE HAPPY ONCE CIRCUMSTANCES CHANGE

Happiness is a state of mind that has nothing to do with circumstances. "Dear Abby" received a letter from a woman complaining about her husband's snoring. In reply, "Dear Abby" quoted a letter from another woman: "I used to complain about snoring. My husband is dead now. I would give anything to be able to hear him snoring again."

An often-told story is the one about struggling newlyweds who do not appreciate the joy of being together and in love because they keep focusing on how much better it will be when they have more money, a house, and furniture. Then they get the money, house, and furniture but don't enjoy them because they think they are not as much in love as they used to be. In fact, they do not experience the joy of love because they keep focusing on circumstances. They cannot see what *is* when focusing on what *is not*. In our thought systems, we want more, better, different. In our hearts, we feel contentment and gratitude.

We experience joy in our relationships when we are unconditionally loving—when we take off our blinders and see our partner the same way we did when we fell in love. You might object, "But my wife is not the same as when we fell in love. She wasn't fat then." The answer to every possible objection can be found in the principles. Your happiness has nothing to do with what anyone else is or does. If you are seeing the fat, you are not seeing the insecurity, which you may have helped create. When you see with *love* instead of with *judgment*, you will also see solutions.

June was miserable because her husband, Cy, was an alcoholic. She vowed to herself that if he did not stop drinking by the time the children left home, she would leave him. They had been married thirty years when the last child left for college. Before June kept her vow, she decided to see a therapist who taught her the principles. She decided to try meditation to see if could receive a message about what to do. She was surprised at the clear inspiration she received from her inner wisdom: "It is not your province to judge your husband but to love him unconditionally." June's reality changed; she loved Cy unconditionally without effort, and within three months he stopped drinking.

Some people have interpreted this story to mean that a woman should deny the problems of alcoholism and become an "enabler" by ignoring the issue. If you have heard the principles with *understanding*, you realize that the story does not set forth a rule; it simply tells what happened to one woman who listened to the inspiration from her inner wisdom. Someone else might hear a totally different message. The message could be to leave with love or to lovingly insist on an intervention program. The possibilities are limitless. Only one thing will always be the same: Positive results are experienced when following your inner wisdom.

MYTH NO. 7: JEALOUSY IS A SIGN OF CARING

Jealousy is created from the ego and is based on the notion that possessiveness will cure feelings of inadequacy.

It is a way of trying to get someone else to take responsibility for your own happiness.

Jealousy, which is based on an illusory feeling of unimportance, is just a form of insecurity produced by thoughts about ego and self-importance. These insecurities usually take the form of a fear of inadequacy, a fear of rejection, or a fear of powerlessness. Many people base their lives on these illusions, wasting time and energy trying to hide their fears or trying to blame themselves or others as the cause of their fears.

Fears of inadequacy take such forms as "I won't be good enough. Someone else will be better than I am. If only I were more beautiful (or handsome, powerful, successful, intelligent, witty), then I would be okay."

Fears of rejection take such forms as "He won't care as much as I care, which means I'm not good enough, so he might leave me, and then I'll be alone and will never find anyone else."

Fears of powerlessness take such forms as "I can't do anything about this. I have no control over what is happening to me. I can't make someone love me."

All these fears are self-worth issues. The belief that anyone can lack self-worth is an illusion based on years of conditioning from childhood. When we *understand* this, we can have compassion for ourselves for buying into the illusion and compassion for those who perpetuated it out of their lack of *understanding*. Before *understanding*, however, the illusions created by the thought system are powerful detours away from happiness in relationships.

Bill and Sue went to a party. When he saw her dancing with another man, he became angry. He sulked on the way home until Sue persuaded him to admit that something was wrong. Then he blew up! He blamed her for flirting and accused her of being inconsiderate. He would not accept her explanation that she didn't especially want to dance with the other man but didn't know how to refuse gracefully.

> Jealousy, which is based on an illusory feeling of unimportance, is just a form of insecurity produced by thoughts about ego and self-importance.

Bill had become so lost in the contents of his thinking that he didn't connect his behavior with his original thoughts of insecurity. He had used blame to cover up his fear that Sue might find him inadequate compared to the other man and that she might decide to reject him—a fear against which he felt powerless. Expressing anger gave him a false sense of power and control—but certainly not happiness.

Bill decided to leave Sue to protect himself from being left by her. He created the very thing he feared in order to protect himself from what he feared.

It is easy for us to see the absurdity when observing the illusions of others. Understanding helps us see the absurdity of our own illusions—with compassion.

MYTH NO. 8: YOU MUST HAVE A RELATIONSHIP

Who says you have to have a relationship?

This is just another belief based on another thought, and when you look at the evidence, it makes no sense.

There are just as many (or more) *un*happy people in relationships as there are happy people in relationships, and there are people who are happy without a relationship as well as unhappy people in the same circumstances.

Again, it's not the circumstances themselves but how you think about them. When you have peace of mind, gratitude, and satisfaction with all that *is*, you don't see what is not. You are happy with or without a relationship.

You can be in love with life, alone as well as with someone.

CHAPTER FIFTEEN

Wisdom—and Lack of Wisdom— from the Ages

Wisdom from the ages makes sense at a deeper level when we understand the principles of thinking as a function, separate realities, levels of consciousness, and feelings as a compass.

IF YOU CAN'T SAY SOMETHING NICE, DON'T SAY ANYTHING AT ALL

Understanding that your reality is a creation of your thoughts rather than the only reality makes it easy to see the wisdom in keeping silent when you have nothing nice to say. It makes no sense to say something nasty or judgmental about other realities. Since negative feelings are simply an indicator of a low mood created by your programmed thought system, it is wise not to say anything at all during that time.

As soon as you dismiss your thought system, seeing or saying something unkind will not be part of your reality. From your heart, you see through the eyes of love and compassion. You know that other people are doing the best they can while seeing the world through the filters of their programmed thought systems.

COUNT TO TEN

Counting to ten is a way of dismissing thought and getting quiet until low moods pass. Some of us may need to count to ten thousand. Looking for life lessons and mirror insight messages can be as effective as counting to ten. When nothing seems to work to pry you loose from your negative thoughts and feelings, you may need help to heal deeply programmed thoughts and beliefs.

TIME HEALS ALL WOUNDS

This is true only when that time is spent in quiet, or at least not thinking about whatever may have caused an emotional wound. Have you ever looked back and felt foolish about getting upset about something that now appears ridiculous and unimportant? Or, have you looked back and realized that what upset you once was truly a blessing "in disguise"? This growth in perspective could be called "growing up," which happens naturally with time.

The thought system can stunt our growth and keep wounds from healing naturally. When we see the world through the filters of our thought systems, we remain stuck in the past instead of experiencing life freshly, moment to moment. Rehashing old wounds is like pouring bacteria in a physical wound: The infection can be worse than the original trauma and can rob time of its power to heal.

Even though the body is designed to heal itself, some physical wounds take longer to heal than others. Likewise, some emotional wounds may take more time to heal than others. *Understanding* the four principles does not mean you will never feel hurt, sad, or angry. You would not be normal if you didn't feel sad over the loss of a loved one, angry at man's inhumanity to man, and hurt when your desires aren't fulfilled. However, even these events feel different when viewed from your heart, where you can feel sadness over your loss, followed by gratitude for the time you had with your loved one; hurt, followed by gratitude for the life lessons you have learned; and anger, followed by compassion, forgiveness, and inner guidance about what to do when something needs to be done. This will include compassion for yourself to take whatever time you need to heal.

HASTE MAKES WASTE

The need to hurry to figure things out keeps you bogged down in your thought system. You gain perspective when you slow down and leave room for inspiration. From your heart or spiritual source, you will find solutions in less time and with no effort. Stop thinking about it (whatever it is), slow down, enjoy life, and watch inspiration flow.

Haste is also a distraction from serenity. In our society, we are inundated with things, and things to do, and places to go. If you find yourself caught up in this haste, go back and read chapter 10 again on getting quiet or simply listen to your heart. Is busyness really what you want? How will you feel about it ten years from now? Will all the things you are doing really matter? Too many people wait for a life-threatening event (or the loss of a loved one) before they realize the most satisfactory way to live their lives. Slow down and listen.

STICKS AND STONES MAY BREAK MY BONES, BUT NAMES WILL NEVER HURT ME

Shari said, "I feel like a failure because my husband tells me I never do anything right. No wonder I don't have any self-esteem."

Shari's sense of failure comes not from her husband's criticisms but from *her thoughts about* them. If Shari would dismiss her thoughts about her husband's comments, from her heart she would know that what he says comes from his separate reality. She would see the innocence and insecurity behind what he is saying.

With *understanding*, Shari would know what to do. Instead of taking his thoughts seriously, she might then feel inspired to hug him, make a joke, take a walk, or whatever her inner wisdom would lead her to do. Have you ever noticed that people tend not to use intimidation with people who don't get hooked by it? When Shari stops getting hooked, her husband might stop. If he doesn't, her inner wisdom can lead her to the next step.

A STITCH IN TIME SAVES NINE

The only stitch we need to take is to *understand* thought, and the trouble that this will save us is greater than nine.

A small tear in a piece of cloth gets larger and larger unless it is stitched while it is still small. In the same way, a negative thought can grow more and more powerful unless it is dismissed as soon as you realize that it is just a thought.

But there is also an interesting difference: When you let a tear in cloth get larger, it takes more work to fix it. Understanding makes it simple to dismiss the thought system. As soon as you recognize a thought for what it is, the negative power is gone. Inspiration from the heart is never work but pleasure.

When you have an intellectual understanding of the principles, have tried getting quiet to wait for them to pass, but still feel stuck in negative thoughts and emotions, don't beat yourself up. Everything is as it should be. Knowing this will keep you open to messages from your inner wisdom. It is not a coincidence that you will find exactly what you need when you are open to guidance from your heart or spiritual source.

An understanding of the principles gives new meaning to many old sayings, but your understanding can also help you see the lack of wisdom in some of the old adages.

IDLENESS IS THE DEVIL'S WORKSHOP

Idleness is not a sin; it leaves room for inspiration. Nevertheless, so many people fear that if they are not constantly busy, they will not be productive.

What is productiveness? Productivity from inspiration produces happiness; productivity from the thought system produces unhappiness. We may be productive in achievement, material prosperity, or a spotless house while our personal family life is falling apart. Or we may be productive trying to find satisfaction outside ourselves and wonder why we never feel satisfied.

Wayne Dyer tells a wonderful story in his tape series *Secrets of the Universe*.[1] Once there were two alley cats. The young cat spent his days frantically chasing his tail. One day the old alley cat wandered by and stopped to watch the young cat. He finally interrupted and asked, "Would you mind telling me what you are doing?"

The young alley cat stopped, took a few minutes to catch his breath, and explained, "I went to cat philosophy school and learned that happiness is in the end of our tails. I know that if I chase long enough and hard enough, I am going to catch a big bite of that happiness."

---

1. Nightingale Conant Corp., The Human Resources Company, Chicago, IL.

The old alley cat reflected, "I have not been to cat philosophy school, but I know it is true that happiness is in the end of our tails. I have observed, however, that if I simply wander around enjoying my life, it follows me everywhere I go."

The way some of us run around in circles trying to be "productive" could be seen as trying to catch a big bite of that happiness somewhere outside ourselves. We could learn much from the wise old alley cat.

> When achieving happiness and peace of mind is your only goal, you will know what to do regardless of what anyone else has ever thought or said.

Actually, it is never *what* we do that matters but rather why we do it and how we feel as we achieve our results. When we are idle because we are happy and want to just enjoy life, we will find more happiness. When we are idle because we are unhappy, depressed, or bored, our discontent grows worse.

It is a popular opinion today that watching television is a waste of time. Maybe so, maybe not. We may watch television as part of our enjoyment of life or as an effort to escape life. Or, we may avoid watching television because we are afraid of what other people will think or because we have adopted the notion that only uneducated people who don't have anything better to do watch television.

The same could be said of any activity or inactivity in life. When achieving happiness and peace of mind is your only goal, you will know what to do regardless of what anyone else has ever thought or said.

*You'll find that happiness lies right under
your eyes back in your own back yard.*

THE ROAD TO HELL IS PAVED
WITH GOOD INTENTIONS

Knowing that people have good intentions can inspire
compassion instead of judgment. When good intentions
fail, it is usually because thought-produced insecurities
create detours.

We all have good intentions to be happy and do the
best we can based on our present level of understanding.
People who commit the most heinous crimes truly "know
not what they do." They are deeply entrenched in a programmed thought system where *understanding* is beyond
their reality.

Forgiveness is easy when we understand the good
intentions of ourselves and others; it is difficult when
we pay attention to the behavior resulting from the

insecurities produced by a distorted thought system. The thought system distorts good intentions and can interpret happiness as money, possessions, fame, power, or anything outside oneself.

People locked into their thought systems and negative behaviors create a kind of hell for themselves. It is our judgments of them that lead to our own kind of hell. The *Course in Miracles* makes this point over and over: "Such is the form of madness you believe, if you accept the fearful though you can attack another and be free yourself."[2]

A PERSON WITHOUT GOALS IS LIKE A SHIP WITHOUT A RUDDER

A person with goals may be like a boat, not without a rudder but with a rudder stuck in one position. Being without goals allows us to enjoy opportunities as they come along. (Actually, goals from the heart will be much different from goals from the thought system.)

The belief that we must have goals often is based on thoughts that create insecurity, such as "Without goals we will never accomplish anything." People who accomplish goals based on those thoughts do not accomplish

> As with everything else, goals are totally different when they come from the heart than when they come from a programmed thought system.

---

2. A *Course in Miracles* (The Foundation for Inner Peace, Glenn Ellen, CA), p. 374.

happiness; instead, they feel only temporary satisfaction and quickly invent new goals.

When we are not focused on goals for the sake of ego reinforcement, we will see opportunities for the sake of enjoyment. Productivity is enhanced through enjoyment. With *understanding*, we want to accomplish only the things that are enhancing to ourselves and others and don't worry about satisfying our egos or other people's expectations.

New Year's resolutions so often fail after a brief spurt of success because it can take too much energy to satisfy the ego. So, many people give up. Success is effortless, however, when following inspiration from the heart.

We often look at someone who is accomplishing something and say, "Wow, she really has self-discipline and sticks to her goals." If you take a closer look, you may often find that she is following not a goal but inspiration. Inspiration provides energy, whereas goals from the thought system drain energy. It is difficult not to follow inspiration, but it can be difficult to muster the energy to pursue goals from other sources.

Lest you start making it a rule not to have goals, when *understanding* takes you to your heart and inner wisdom, you may receive inspiration that leads you to a goal. As with everything else, goals are totally different when they come from the heart than when they come from a programmed thought system.

Deepak Chopra describes the difference between coming from the thought system or the heart when he writes, "Learn to harness the power of intention, and you can create anything you desire. You can still get results through effort and through trying, but at a cost. The cost is stress, heart attacks, and the compromised function of your immune system."[3]

ANYTHING WORTH DOING IS WORTH DOING WELL

The maxim "Anything worth doing is worth doing well" may be true if "well" simply means that you enjoy doing it, but "well" is usually a judgment, with implications of perfection. Beliefs about perfection often take the joy out of doing.

How many people will not sing for the fun of it because they feel that they cannot sing well enough? This is just one example of the many things people avoid doing for pleasure because they're afraid they won't live up to the judgment of doing it "well."

Anything worth doing is worth doing for the fun of it!

GROWTH IS PAINFUL

It is true that what is referred to as growth within the thought system is painful. Delving into the past for reasons or excuses, expressing feelings of anger based on blame, and controlling emotions are the kinds of growth that can be very painful. The pain is unnecessary.

---

3. Deepak Chopra, *The Seven Laws of Spiritual Success* (San Rafael, CA: Amber-Allen Publishing & New World Library, 1994), pp. 75–76.

Growth based on inspiration from your heart is not painful. It is painless to dismiss thoughts on which the pain is based.

Healing programmed thoughts and beliefs is helpful only when it releases the pain and leaves room for love and compassion. We feel content when we see life with understanding, but it keeps getting better because our understanding continues to grow and deepen. There is nothing painful about it.

IT'S TOO GOOD TO BE TRUE

The only thing that can take away the goodness in something is negative thoughts. Think it, and you have it. If you think that the goodness can't last, you have already started to create misery instead of enjoying what is.

If we think something can't last, it is because we have quit enjoying what is and have adopted thoughts such as "I can't be happy if I don't have this" or "It might not last" or "I don't deserve it."

It is true that "it" might not last. So what? Becoming attached to it just keeps you from seeing so much more.

GOOD THINGS ALWAYS COME TO AN END

When we think, "Good things always come to an end," we have put on our blinders so we can't see the abundance of good things. Good things don't come to an end until we change our thoughts and start worrying about the past or future and stop enjoying *what is*. When we see the abundance of good things, it makes no sense to worry about losing one good thing.

From your heart, you will see what is with gratitude. There is always something to be grateful for.

Life is good.

CHAPTER SIXTEEN

Keys to Happiness:
A Summary

Would you like to be in prison? Would you knowingly confine yourself to a life sentence in a dungeon? These questions may sound ridiculous at first, but perhaps you have felt at times as though you've locked yourself in a kind of prison without realizing it. You may feel the confinement of the life you have created without being aware that it is your creation.

Your thought system creates a prison as confining as any dungeon. The prison walls you create in your mind are formed from illusionary thoughts, but they can be as binding as concrete.

The foundation stones for a prison of illusions are made of thoughts that create feelings of insecurity. The walls are made of whatever form the insecurity takes—self-importance, drinking, anxiety, overeating, judgment, overachievement, expectations, stress, dissatisfaction,

depression, blame. The ceiling is the belief that these thoughts are reality.

THE PRINCIPLES AS KEYS TO HAPPINESS

An *understanding* of the principles we have discussed in previous chapters is the master key to the prison doors. Know the truth, and the truth shall make you free.

There can be a wide chasm, however, between intellectual knowledge and experiential reality. Intellectually, I believed that happiness came from within, but I did not understand the barriers that kept me from experiencing the truth of the knowledge. An *understanding* of the four principles provided the treasure map that led me past the barriers to my inner happiness. They are summarized here.

Thinking as a Function

The foundation principle is realizing that *thinking is a function*. This realization is the key to experiencing natural mental health and inner happiness. Those who believe wholly in the contents of their thinking often experience stress, anxiety, and other forms of insecurity. They take negative thoughts seriously, turn them into beliefs, and live for them. They have created perception prisons.

Those who understand that thinking is a function experience freedom and serenity. By seeing the humor in their negative creations and therefore not taking them seriously, they are able to dismiss negativity and experience natural well-being from their hearts or spiritual sources. They have unlocked the prison doors.

Feelings as a Compass

The principle of *using our feelings as a compass* is the tool that lets us know where we are on our treasure map. Anytime we are feeling bad, we have forgotten that thinking is a function, and therefore we are seeing our thoughts as reality. Anytime we are feeling unconditional love, joy, gratitude, or compassion, the treasure is no longer buried; we are living from our hearts and inner wisdom.

Separate Realities

When we understand the principle of *separate realities*, we see differences with interest and compassion rather than with judgment. Compassion does not mean we approve of every action by others; it means we understand their insecurity and lack of *understanding*. We often ignore the fact that we have made ourselves miserable with our judgments and forget that serenity is just a dropped thought away. When we see others with interest and compassion, it is because we are living from our hearts.

Mood Levels

The principle of *mood levels*, or *levels of consciousness*, is closely related to the others. We are in a low mood or level of consciousness when we forget that thinking is a function, when we forget to respect separate realities, when we forget to use our compass as a guide, and especially when we try to use our thought system to find a solution to our predicament. An *understanding* of this principle implies a higher level of consciousness, which will lead us to compassion for ourselves while we wait for a low mood to pass. Persistent low moods may be giving us the message that we need to seek help to heal troubling thoughts and beliefs from a deeply programmed thought system.

> A key to this prison door is to give up the belief that circumstances dictate our happiness and to see that our serenity has everything to do with how we view circumstances.

BARRIERS TO HAPPINESS

Between intellectual knowledge and experiential understanding of the principles, however, are barriers created in our thought system that can keep us from our inner happiness and serenity.

Circumstances

It is never the circumstances but our thoughts about them that create our state of mind. We can always find examples of people who have maintained their peace of mind under the very circumstances we think are causing us to feel awful, and many books have been written about their inspiring stories.

Refusing to understand this truth is what keeps people imprisoned in their judgments, in the hopelessness of a victim mentality and the bitterness of unforgiveness. A key to this prison door is to give up the belief that circumstances dictate our happiness and to see that our serenity has everything to do with how we view circumstances. Another key is to remember that positive thinking is not the answer. Seeing through your heart is.

Judgments

We judge others when we forget about separate realities and delude ourselves that our reality is the right one. For everything we judge, someone else has been able to see the same event with compassion and understanding. Judgment is similar to the pot calling the kettle black or "looking for the mote in the eye of another, when the beam in our own eye distorts our view."

When we observe others through our judgment filters, we are defining our own state of mind even while believing that we are defining theirs. The person we are judging may be blinded by insecurity or some other form of negativity, but if we were not blind ourselves, we would see their innocence and realize that person just doesn't know better. Instead of judgment, we would feel compassion and understanding; we might then be inspired to do something to make that person feel more secure or else we might stop judging them and get out of their way.

A key that can release you from your judgments is to "look in the mirror." What "fault" of your own is reflected in your judgments? The prison door opens only when you see your own faults with compassion. What a gift it can be to see our own faults in others. What might have been blind to us before is seen clearly when we see it in others and acknowledge the reflection.

Expectations

When we are focused on expectations, we can be blind to the beauty and wonders right in front of us. Therefore, whenever we narrow our vision to expecting certain outcomes, we greatly increase the probability of disappointment.

A key to happiness is to give up our expectations so we can see and enjoy *what is*. Remember: There are miracles all around us, in every moment. When living life from our hearts, we *see* the miracles and are filled with gratitude.

Assumptions

Assuming that we know what someone else is thinking or experiencing is a mistake. We have missed a deep understanding of the principle of separate realities when we give credibility to our assumptions. When we base our thoughts and feelings on assumptions, we react to our assumptions and blame others for what we think they think. It can be humorous when we see it.

Wayne Dyer tells a story about a woman who believed she was inadequate because her husband said she was. Wayne asked, "If your husband said you were a car, would that make you a car?" She replied, "Of course not." Wayne pushed, "Wait a minute. What if he tried to put gas in your ear; then would you believe you are a car?" She laughed, "No, I'm not a car." Wayne concluded, "Then why would you believe you are inadequate? Obviously he can't make you believe anything you choose not to believe."

A key to happiness is to give up our assumptions and the assumptions of others and live life freshly, moment to moment, from our heart and inner wisdom.

Beliefs and Realities

Alfred Adler once said, "Ideas have no meaning except the meaning we give them." We often attach such importance to the meaning we assign to our thoughts and ideas that they become beliefs we live and die for.

A firm belief in the flatness of the world does not make it so. Believing that because water is clear it is free of microorganisms doesn't mean they are not there.

A key to happiness is remembering that beliefs and realities are creations of our thoughts. Most of our

> It is impossible to feel gratitude and negativity at the same time.

thoughts were programmed when we couldn't see the truth, just as we can't see that the world is round. The truth that we find in our hearts and inner wisdom can free us from the beliefs we created.

SIGNPOSTS TO HAPPINESS

Signposts on our treasure map provide keys to help us get past the barriers of our thought systems to the experiential reality of our inner happiness and serenity.

Gratitude

Joe: "I can't see anything to be grateful for in this messed-up world."

Wise old Zeke: "I'll bet you would be a millionaire if I gave you $100 for everything you could think of to be grateful for."

You will see what you look for.

Gratitude is a natural feeling when the thought system has been dismissed. In higher levels of consciousness, we see that the beauty of life is all around us, and we are filled with gratitude. When we are grateful, we see how silly it is to be upset by some of the little things we take seriously in a lower state of mind.

When first learning about the principles, I felt disappointed in myself every time I got lost in thought. As my understanding increased, I stopped taking this seriously and had compassion for myself. Now I even feel a sense of gratitude when I get lost because I know I will come out of it with greater understanding. Every time I get off track and experience my judgments or any other form of negativity, the experience confirms that being lost in thought is not a pleasant place to be, and my understanding deepens.

It is impossible to feel gratitude and negativity at the same time. My understanding of that truth lets me know that it makes sense to focus on what I am grateful for rather than on what I have been thinking about to make myself unhappy.

Gratitude is my favorite key.

Compassion

Feeling compassion is another natural occurrence when we see what thought is. With perspective, we see the innocence in others and know that they do the very best they can from their present level of understanding.

A key to happiness is allowing ourselves to experience the compassion from our heart; that makes it easy to forgive ourselves as well as others.

What We See (or Feel or Give) Is What We Get

When we are in a low mood and feeling judgmental or angry, we are stuck with those feelings. When we are in a high mood and see the innocence of all behaviors, we have feelings of love, compassion, and understanding; we have peace of mind. When we give love, that is what we get.

L ove and *under-standing* are the same thing.

We don't have to get it from someone else because love is inherent in the feelings we have when we give love.

A key to happiness is understanding that we reap what we sow.

Love and Understanding

The greatest key of all is love. When we feel loving, we see beauty and goodness in everything—or at least, we see the perfection of all things. All that is needed to solve any problem we can imagine is love.

Love and *understanding* are the same thing. Love without understanding is conditional (not love at all). With understanding, it is impossible to judge; with understanding, we have compassion; with understanding, we have peace of mind and contentment; with understanding, we have love.

Remember that *understanding* is not about "shoulds." Suppose you don't feel loving—so what? You feel what you feel based on your present level of understanding. "Shoulding" on yourself about that just makes it worse. Understanding usually changes what you feel, but if you try to change it through "shoulds," you block understanding.

A key to happiness is listening to your inner wisdom until understanding sneaks past your thought system.

The Battle Between Love and Ego

Love is the ultimate reality; ego is the ultimate illusion. Ego is the need to prove self-importance, which is based on the illusory belief in insecurity. It is the source of jealousy, self-righteousness, possessiveness, judgment, expectation, revenge, depression, stress, and disease.

What power this illusion of ego can create.

But love has a greater power: Love heals every problem. Through the perspective of love, problems disappear. Love fills us with feelings that guide us to solutions that make the problem seem insignificant.

Joe chided Zeke, "All this talk of love sounds like religion and the flower children from the sixties to me. It really turns me off."

Wise old Zeke replied, "Could it be that the reason you don't have much love in your life is because it turns you off?"

A key to happiness is recognizing the difference between love and ego so that ego can be dismissed and love can be enjoyed.

Enjoying *What Is* While It Is

Have you ever looked back at a time in your life and thought, "I was really happy then. Too bad I didn't appreciate it more at the time"? Have you known others who thought that their circumstances were a tragedy but later saw them as the best thing that ever happened to them? This is an example of the perfection of all things. We may not be able to understand the perfection at the moment, unless we have understanding.

When we understand the principles, the beauty of life is profound. What used to seem ordinary or insignificant is seen with appreciation and gratitude. We are often so filled with beauty, contentment, and the wonder of life that we have no choice except to get quiet and enjoy it.

A key to happiness is to enjoy what is.

Happiness and Serenity

What could be more important than happiness and serenity? When happiness is what we want, it makes no sense to entertain thoughts that lead in any other direction

Can you imagine the wonderful revolution that will take place when we all start dismissing the many thoughts that create so much misery?

This key to happiness is so simple. Dismiss negative thoughts, and you have happiness and serenity.

As a man thinketh, so is he.

Index

ABOUT THE AUTHOR

 JANE NELSEN is a popular lecturer and coauthor of the entire POSITIVE DISCIPLINE series. She has appeared on *Oprah* and *Sally Jesse Raphael* and was the featured parent expert on the *National Parent Quiz*, hosted by Ben Vereen. Jane is the mother of seven children and the grandmother of seventeen.

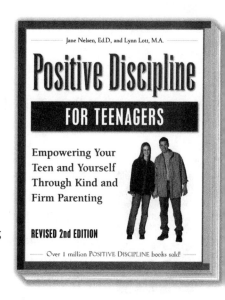

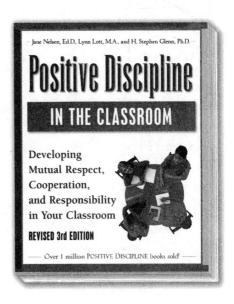

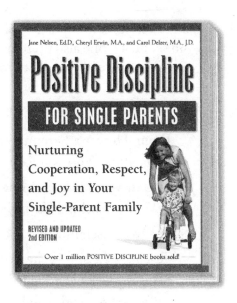

FOR MORE INFORMATION

Jane Nelsen is a popular keynote speaker for conferences and seminars. She also presents dynamic workshops for corporations, parents, teachers, and other professionals who work with children.

Topics include:

From Here to Serenity: Four Principles for Understanding Who You Really Are

Fifteen Ways to Avoid Power Struggles With Children While Teaching Valuable Life Skills

Positive Discipline in the Classroom

Teaching Parenting the Positive Discipline Way
(This workshop is designed for facilitator training for parent educators and may have a specific focus for parents of preschoolers, parents of teenagers, parents of children ages six to twelve, or parents in recovery.)

Jane can be contacted through:
Empowering People
P. O. Box 1926
Orem, Utah 84059
1-800-456-7770
www.positivediscipline.com
call 1-800-456-7770.

ORDER FORM

To: Empowering People, P.O. Box 1926, Orem UT 84059
Phone: 1-800-456-7770 (credit card orders only)
Fax: 801-762-0022
Web site: www.positivediscipline.com

BOOKS	Price	Quantity	Amount
From Here to Serenity by Nelsen	$14.00		
Positive Time-Out by Nelsen	$12.00		
Positive Discipline by Nelsen	$11.00		
Raising Self-Reliant Children in a Self-Reliant World by Glenn & Nelsen	$12.95		
Positive Discipline: The First Three Years by Nelsen, Erwin, & Duffy	$16.00		
Positive Discipline for Preschoolers by Nelsen, Erwin, & Duffy	$16.00		
Positive Discipline for Teenagers by Nelsen & Lott	$16.95		
Positive Discipline A–Z by Nelsen, Lott, & Glenn	$16.00		
Positive Discipline for Single Parents by Nelsen, Erwin, & Delzer	$16.00		
Positive Discipline for Blended Families by Nelsen, Erwin, & Glenn	$15.00		
Positive Discipline for Parenting in Recovery by Nelsen, Lott, & Intner	$12.95		
Positive Discipline in the Classroom by Nelsen, Lott, & Glenn	$16.95		
Positive Discipline: A Teacher's A–Z Guide by Nelsen, Duffy, Escobar, Ortolano, & Owen-Sohocki	$14.95		

TAPES AND VIDEOS			
Positive Discipline cassette tape	$10.00		
Positive Discipline video	$49.95		
Building Healthy Self-Esteem Through Positive Discipline cassette tape	$10.00		

SUBTOTAL _____

Sales tax: UT add 6.25%; CA add 7.25% _____

Shipping & handling: $2.50 plus $0.50 each item _____

TOTAL _____

(Prices subject to change without notice.)

METHOD OF PAYMENT (check one):
_____ Check made payable to Empowering People Books, Tapes, & Videos
_____ MasterCard, Visa, Discover Card, American Express

Card # _____ Expiration _____ / _____

Ship to _____

Address _____

City/State/Zip _____

Daytime phone _____ (_____) _____